SPECIAL PRAISE FOR

How to Be Perfect Like Me

"Dana Bowman's writing is luminous, laugh-out-loud wondrous and makes something profound shift within, much like staring saucer-eyed at a field full of fireflies. While we do approach recovery differently, that didn't matter; I related to her hugely and rooted hard for her throughout. This big-hearted book rejoices in the messy, tangled clusterf*ck of being a perfectly imperfect human."

—CATHERINE GRAY, AUTHOR OF *The Unexpected Joy of Being Sober*

"Dana Bowman is honest, insightful, and incredibly funny, which is hard, especially as she tries to love herself. Men, don't be surprised if your wife hands you this book and says, 'Read this, and then maybe you'll understand.'"

—STAN FRIEDMAN, WRITER AND EDITOR FOR THE *Covenant Companion*

"Real, honest, hopeful, and funny. That is what I love about Dana Bowman's writing, and her second book does not disappoint. *How to Be Perfect Like Me* is like spreading all your issues out on the kitchen table and laugh-crying at them over a good cup of tea. Highly recommended for women who are ready to know that every one of us struggles, but that struggle is just the beginning of the story."

—ALISON BUEHLER, AUTHOR OF *Rethinking Women's Health*

How to
❧ **Be Perfect** ☙
Like Me

HOW

❊ TO BE ❊

perfect

LIKE

me

Dana
Bowman

CRP
CENTRAL RECOVERY PRESS
Las Vegas

Central Recovery Press (CRP) is committed to publishing exceptional materials addressing addiction treatment, recovery, and behavioral healthcare topics.

For more information, visit www.centralrecoverypress.com.

Publisher: Central Recovery Press
       3321 N. Buffalo Drive
       Las Vegas, NV 89129

23 22 21 20 19 18   1 2 3 4 5

Photo of Dana Bowman by Erica Heline. Used with permission.

Library of Congress Cataloging-in-Publication Data
Names: Bowman, Dana, author.
Title: How to be perfect like me / Dana Bowman.
Description: Las Vegas, NV : Central Recovery Press, 2018.
Identifiers: LCCN 2017056276 (print) | LCCN 2017058771 (ebook) | ISBN
  9781942094722 (ebook) | ISBN 9781942094715 (pbk. : alk. paper)
Subjects: LCSH: Bowman, Dana. | Recovering alcoholics--Biography. |
  Motherhood--Humor. | Conduct of life--Humor.
Classification: LCC HV5137 (ebook) | LCC HV5137 .B692 2018 (print) | DDC
  362.292092 [B] --dc23
LC record available at https://lccn.loc.gov/2017056276

Every attempt has been made to contact copyright holders. If copyright holders have not been properly acknowledged, please contact us. Central Recovery Press will be happy to rectify the omission in future printings of this book.

Publisher's Note: This book contains general information about addiction, addiction recovery, and related matters. The information is not medical advice. This book is not an alternative to medical advice from your doctor or other professional healthcare provider.

Our books represent the experiences and opinions of their authors only. Every effort has been made to ensure that events, institutions, and statistics presented in our books as facts are accurate and up-to-date. To protect their privacy, the names of some of the people, places, and institutions in this book may have been changed.

Cover and interior design and layout by Marisa Jackson

To Brian
Thank you for the ruckus.

And to Mom & Dad
Because everyone should have a Julie.
And we all really need a Jim.

TABLE OF

contents

"This above all: to thine own self be true."
—WILLIAM SHAKESPEARE

"Lord, what fools these mortals be!"
—SAME GUY

It took a wedding, two babies, and a funeral to help me understand that I needed to get sober. And I survived parenting those same two babies while in recovery.

But, as I found, being in recovery has little to do with not drinking. How I survive being *me* is another story.

I am standing in the same classroom where I completely fell apart six years ago. It's the classroom where I tried to teach seventh graders not to use an exclamation mark after each sentence when they write! The falling apart happened because I drank too much, not because of all those exclamation marks! Although—who knows!? Perhaps this whole thing started because of willy-nilly punctuation!

Back when I was drinking, I often behaved like a seventh grader—tons of drama and a lot of exclamation marks all over the place, usually in ways that didn't make much sense. I think there were a couple of times I tried to break up with my husband via text.

And now I am back at ground zero, staring around my old classroom like I'm at an art exhibit and my life is on display. My classroom used to be cute, but it has been taken over by a football coach, and there are no Scentsy warmers or soft lighting. The room smells like pencil erasers and stale Fruit Roll-Ups. Later, when the class piles in, fresh from PE, it will smell much worse. I don't mind.

This time around, I am a substitute teacher. When I was teaching full time, I thought substitute teaching was a sort of Walmart-greeter no-man's-land with one job: to smile, wave, and feebly say welcome as the throngs pass by. You are a door holder until the real teacher returns.

But, as the universe would have it, my subbing days have been rather wonderful. I swoop in, mess with a teacher's lesson plans, and then swoop out again. I subbed for a kindergarten class and sang "We're So Glad You're Here." Their enthusiasm was on a par with an *American Idol* audition, and the cuteness nearly brought tears to my eyes. In another classroom with fourth graders, I taught long division to a kid who had decided long division was going to break him. "Not on my watch, kid," I growled. "Let's *do* this." And by God, we did long division.

I administer Band-Aids, play four square at recess, and flit in and out of the schools in my little town with reckless, poorly paid abandon. The job is not linked to any big and important thing that I have to do. It's just *fun*. How can you not have fun when your day involves reading *How to Eat Fried Worms* to third graders and then talking about King Tut? Shouldn't everyone live like this?

But on this day, I have been assigned a gig back in my old school. So far, I have only worked at the elementary school because they have Teddy Grahams snacks, and I can still play the Mom Card. Plus, they have a therapy dog. She walks along with her owner, a big dog smile on her face, and all the little hands reach out and touch her fur as they walk past, single file.

The middle school has no therapy dog. This is odd, because if anyone needs a therapy dog, it's preteens and their teachers. But the middle school called and asked if I could come in, and, dog or not, here I am. I wonder, should I be messed up about this? Should I be sad? Does anyone smell the layers of alcohol in the walls that wafted off me here? Is there any sort of sign that I ever was in this room, in a different life? In a different mind?

Where is that therapy dog when you need her?

All I can smell is a whole lot of Axe layered on seventh-grade boys. If that's not going to drive you to drink, I don't know what is.

However, it didn't.

Because I'm Dana . . . and I'm an alcoholic . . . and I don't drink anymore.

But, as always, there is more to the story.

less

"Take some more tea," the March Hare said to Alice, very earnestly.

"I've had nothing yet," Alice replied in an offended tone, "so I can't take more."

"You mean you can't take less," said the Hatter; "it's very easy to take more than nothing."

"Nobody asked your opinion," said Alice.

—LEWIS CARROLL

CHAPTER ONE

HOW TO

be perfect

"What's wrong?" my husband asked, standing next to me. He seemed perturbed. He was also holding a garish fluff of cotton candy about the size of a small toddler. It's kind of tough to look irritated when holding pink cotton candy, but that was how the day had gone. We were at the citywide fair, and generally this was a happy place. Cotton candy. A Ferris wheel. The salty tang of popcorn.

However, on this day my son Henry was losing his mind.

Henry, in general, is an affable fellow. I have a lot of cute pictures to prove this in which he is smiling: in his bouncy seat, wearing spaghetti, or riding the dog. (Note: Dog was not smiling.) But when Henry gets upset, he gets Chernobyl upset: the initial blowup is catastrophic, there's no reversal of the effects, and nobody ever wants to go back there and revisit the carnage. Then, as the mushroom cloud erupts from Henry, you can hear some Russian being spoken.

"I THREW MY BALLS AT THE TARGET AND GOT NOTHING, NOTTA ONE THING, NOT AT ALL ANNNNNNNND CHARLIE HAS A PURPLE LION AND I DON'T IT'S NOT FAIRRRRRR *DO SVIDANIYA!*"

When presented with a child who is wailing because he did not win a purple lion made in Pakistan, I go for calm and mystical.

I bent down, gently placing both hands on either side of his tear-streaked cheeks, and said, "Henry. Let's go. I see McDonald's in your future."

Meanwhile, Charlie, the owner of the purple lion breaking Henry's heart, started slowly waving Mr. Cheapo Lion up and down because Charlie is a straight-up dream crusher. This made Henry dial up his amperage. Even the carnival workers looked alarmed, and I assumed those folks already had a pretty high tolerance for that sort of thing.

"IT'S NOT FAIR HE HAS A LION I WANNA TRY FOR THE LION THE LIONNN I WANT ONE AND THE BROTHERS KARAMAZOV!"

The fair was supposed to be a fun family event. You know the ones. There are balloons and fried food and a lot of walking. Sometimes there's tinkly calliope music involved. Fun family events are . . . fun. At least, that is what we parents expected when we signed up for this gig. But, as most parents will tell you, children are the stone-cold killers of expectations.

Granted, the day was hot, and both boys had been in the bouncy castle long enough to rattle their soft little brains into mush. But still, this fun family event was not supposed to end with one kid sobbing so hard he shot cotton candy out of his nose. As God is my witness, I will never be able to get that visual out of my head: Henry's snot suddenly turning electric pink. That kind of memory *stays*.

This is what kids do. We offer an Easter egg hunt, and they eat too many chocolate eggs and puke on their brother. We set up a gigantic, battery-eating Thomas the Train set for Christmas morning, and they throw Thomas at their brother, slicing his forehead and killing Thomas, as well as any hopes of a photogenic moment for the next hour.

These are the tapes that parents play. It's automatic, this search for the happy family moment. We drive past a diner and, without thinking, we say, "Hey, kids! How'd you like to go get an ice cream cone?"

They eye you in the rearview mirror and coolly make a counteroffer. "What, no banana split sundae? Because I want *that*. Not the gruel you just mentioned. Basically, I'm an ungrateful child and I exist to take the wind out of your parenting sails every day. Yep. That's my job."

When I got married, my dad told me to have no expectations. I mean literally, as we walked down the aisle, me in my gown and veil, all glowy and excited. He was doing a Vulcan death grip on my elbow and urgently whispered, "No expectations. Remember that." It seemed like a funny time to offer this counsel. I was confused. This was one of those special moments between a father and a daughter, yet he was giving me really depressing advice.

Based on my informal scientific research, the more depressing the advice is, the more likely it is to be spot-on. And my dad's "no expectations" comment stands. If we humans could actually *do* the whole no-expectations thing, we might be a whole lot happier. If you're asked to think about why you were put here on this earth, often you will try to drum up some really great reasons. "To serve others," you say. "To keep the earth clean," you add. "Oh, and to sell a lot of stuff to make money!" And from there on, it's a free-for-all. "To have a lot of sex! To keep up with the Kardashians! And Lord, once and for all, to fold a fitted sheet!"

If we are really honest with ourselves, it sounds super nice to be all Eagle Scout about it and serve others, but really? What do we really, really *want*? To paraphrase the lyrical musings of the Spice Girls, what we want, what we really, really want is to be *happy*.

Happiness is possible if we are able to have absolutely *no* expectations of *anyone*. Unfortunately, this is impossible. We can't help ourselves. We expect people to use their blinkers when they change lanes. We expect them to not post pictures of their mole removal. We expect them to be on time and wear deodorant.

Starting with the blinker thing, people don't ever do what we want.

Attaining happiness means, really, that everyone and everything around us must be perfect. We would never admit this because it sounds demanding and kind of crazy, like we decided to swim in Lake Me for a little too long and came out all prune-y and unable to adult.

It's true.

Really.

Think about it. Our whole lives have been spent under the false pretense that happiness, or at least a medium sense of well-being, is something that bubbles up from the inside. Yet I would hazard to guess that even the most random moments of chill occur when someone comes by and offers us a jelly doughnut. Maybe happiness isn't some sort of internal spring. Maybe it's a symptom of all the people, places, and oh-so-many things around us. And if you want to contest my theory and tell me that your version of happiness is not influenced by others—good for you—go walk on water somewhere else.

I know. It makes me sound shallow. The thing is, I thought I had this whole "lower your expectations" thing figured out when I got married. It was annoying, at times, to realize my husband was never going to behave exactly as I had planned, but I saw him for about six hours a day, and half of that time we were eating or watching television, so I was allowed breaks. But then, I had children. Children don't do breaks. They have it written in their contract that they will hover around you for as long as you let them—and even when you don't—with the sole purpose of messing with you. Plus, Brian and I had met when we were adults, but I know for a fact I have been with both my boys since birth, so shouldn't they be totally molded and formed and perfected by *moi*?

As one who has witnessed a son burp so hard it actually made him shoot back from the table, I can officially say my children don't do perfect.

I don't really know what I was thinking when I had children, and afterward, for quite some time, I thought there must have been a mistake. At the actual blessed event, I remember thinking, "This totally hurts. If they roll me over again on this table like a whale with wires attached, I'm gonna puke on someone, and I have never done that before." My prediction was spot-on: I actually did puke on my husband while in the middle of contractions that attacked only one side of my body—due to an epidural that went rogue—so that memory is forever with us.

When I had Charlie, the universe visited and cooed at the baby for a minute, and then it smacked me on the back with a smirk and said, "Good luck with this one. He's going to have colic and weird skin stuff, and there will be fluids, so many fluids. Oh, and when he hits five, he will start on his four-year plan to take over the world. Bon voyage!" And then, the universe sauntered off.

⸎

How can we be happy and perfect, all at the same time? We have to accomplish the impossible task of making sure that everything and everyone around us, even those beloved little grimy children, are on board with perfection, too.

If you have ever watched your child attempt to clean up his own mess, you've seen the colossally imperfect in action—a living, breathing metaphor about life's failings, standing right in front of you, wiping so listlessly at the smashed corn flakes on the table, he might as well sculpt them into some artwork on his place mat and call it good. You've seen him achieve a master's and a doctorate in imperfection within minutes of handing him a washcloth because that's when his hand loses all gripping power, and he has forgotten how to speak English. If this creature has been attached to your hip for days on end, then there is simply NO WAY perfection can happen. And thus, happiness is off the table, too. But not the smashed and solidified corn flakes. Those corn flakes are *forever.*

For those of you who don't have children yet and believe you are immune, there are two problems with this thinking: (1) Adults often act like toddlers—and they are at your workplace right now—so you are still screwed. (2) There is a direct correlation between any sort of superior, parental attitude and how totally inept your kid will be once he or she comes barreling out of you. If you dare think, "Well, *my* kid will clean up, blah, blah, blah," you'll get socked with a kid who *won't* with such skill you'll think you've given birth to a baby sloth. You'll even catch yourself checking under his arms for moss.

Initially, after my kids came along, trying for order and control seemed so hard that I gave up. I shrugged and decided to wade into imperfection with an "I'm just gonna let it all hang out" attitude on overdrive. It was a really slow-moving, hazards-flashing, mediocre overdrive, but still. This apathy lasted long enough for me to kind of go crazy. I think it happened the day I found half a mini-Snickers in my couch, under some cushions, and I looked at it long and hard before I decided to throw it out. There was gray fluff all over it, and I was turning it around in my hands like some sort of chocolate-covered artifact that might be edible. I wasn't even hungry. Oh, no. Slow-moving, lumpy mothers don't get hungry. We're too busy eating our kids' gnawed-on leftover cheese sticks for that. And, at that very moment, I considered eating the fluffy Snickers because that was the best method of cleaning it up.

It was a wake-up call. I shook myself and decided that I had to speed up, fly right, get in gear—insert any other transport industry metaphor you can think of. This I did like an infantry tank, mowing over anything in my path and hunting down any sense of control possible.

Even the cats weren't safe from my frenetic pace. I was vacuuming out the couch and poor, hapless Steve happened to amble by. Steve does not fear the vacuum, or much else for that matter, but on this occasion it became his flaw. He ended up lying on his side, looking at me as if to say, "Really? It's come to this?" as I vacuumed his large, fluffy, white tummy.

By the way, this kind of back-and-forth behavior is called the Nutball Pendulum of Despair. It means you either will end up being hospitalized or should run for office. Take your pick. And raising your children puts all that oscillation on high speed.

☙

Recently, after a long, rather forgettable Saturday of endless nothing and laundry, I made a mediocre pasta dinner and three huge bowls of buttery popcorn, and we all sat down to watch *Stuart Little*. And as I sat there with my boys on either side, eating popcorn for dinner and ignoring the pasta, I realized this was awesome. It had been an awesome day. Also, it had been a totally uneventful day. Somehow, those two things were linked. There had been no major mishaps, no crying, and at the same time, no big plans. There had been food and water. There had been twenty-seven games of Crazy Eights. It hadn't gone down as the most memorable day ever, but that's good. That's what made it good.

That's what made it perfect.

I like to think that perfection is elusive because we are looking in the wrong place. We must shift our focus. Instead of looking for perfection in ourselves and others, all we really need to do is look someplace more realistic—like the movies.

How to Be
Perfect in Five Easy Steps

1. Start by rolling enormous rocks up steep hills.

2. Run a lot. Run to the store for organic things.
   Run forgotten lunchboxes back to school.
   Run, smile, and wave.

3. Silently watch your six-year-old attempt to tie
   his shoes with only two minutes to get to class.
   Make no sudden moves. You've got this.

4. Watch a lot of HGTV, especially the shows about
   transforming a split-level ranch into Downton Abbey.
   Wander around your house a lot afterward.

5. Peer at yourself in the mirror, preferably one of
   those magnify-the-heck-out-of-your-pores kinds.
   Repeat as necessary.

CHAPTER TWO

HOW TO
stop buying
ALL THE
self-help books

I've seen *Showgirls*. In fact, I've seen it twice. And one time, I was even sober.

For those of you who don't know, *Showgirls* is a magical little movie in which Elizabeth Berkley shows us all of her skin while simultaneously tanking her career. You remember Elizabeth Berkley, don't you? The spandexed teen star from the television show *Saved by the Bell*? She also plays the superachiever in *Showgirls,* but this time she is a feisty dancer with a dream. This dream involves becoming a showgirl—thus the title—in Las Vegas and snarling at anyone who gets in her way. Also, a whole lot of body glitter is employed. And yes, I really can't explain how I ended up sitting through this movie twice.

However, I have to hand it to Elizabeth. I get her. I also would have liked to hand her a cardigan because she had to be chilly; she wore string and glitter for 80 percent of the movie. And the thing is, the movie . . . it's awful. The whole thing is simply terrible. But all through it, Elizabeth overacts her tiny, glittered butt off. In one scene, she yells at her boss after he calls her, quite accurately, a stripper.

"Hey!" she barks. "I am a DANCER." There is enough fiery indignation in her words to almost set her teeny-tiny feathered costume alight. She is *committed*.

This is how I want to live my life: when everything around you is falling apart, and the script is laughable, pretend you're a showgirl. Own it. Put on some gold eyelashes and wrap a feather boa around you and start shimmying.

I am a lousy mom at times, but I still hear Elizabeth and her insistence and I echo it. "Hey! I am a MOTHER," I exclaim as I get the kids to school five minutes late, and one of them has his pants on backward. "Don't you know who I AM?" I snarl as I offer something brown and sticky for dinner. "I am a MOM, and this is MY rodeo. Now, eat. Later, I will let you watch too much television, and one of you will overhear me using questionable language. And that's just fine. Know why? BECAUSE I AM SLAYING IT HERE." Shimmy, shimmy, shimmy.

I admit this kind of attitude takes a lot of energy. There are times when the recitation of my lines does not quite have Elizabeth's verve. She wears short-shorts with cowboy boots, for Pete's sake, a look no one over thirty-five can pull off unless it's Halloween. Even then, it's debatable. Elizabeth is young, and she has really good abdominal muscles. I am not so young, so at times I lose my conviction. But I press on. "I am a mother," I mutter as the boys behave like feral cats at the grocery store. "I am slaying it here," I sigh as I toss sugar-coated Sucrose O's into the cart.

The *Showgirls* system works. It really does. Case in point: I embraced my inner Elizabeth Berkley when I was newly sober. Early sobriety was pretty much an opportunity for me to fail on a minute-by-minute basis, but for some reason, *Showgirls* pulled me through. "Hey! I am SOBER," I proclaimed as I passed by twenty thousand liquor stores on my way home from errands. "I am IN RECOVERY," I said as I strutted past the gleaming bar in front of our local restaurant, trailing glitter behind me. I would often pair all these dramatic exhortations with jazz hands and a few hip thrusts, just to keep it interesting. No one will mess with you when you turn down a glass of wine and then drop to the floor, do a twisty spin move, and stare seductively.

Okay, granted, most of this was in my imagination, but whatever. I now dial up the *Showgirls* system whenever I am lacking in confidence. If someone asks me what I do for a living, I don't pause and stammer and say, "Well, I write, but just sort of as a hobby, you know? And I have cats." Now, I prance forward in five-inch Lucite heels and growl, "Me? I am an AUTHOR. Remember this face, sweetie, because I am gonna ROCK your nighttime reading routine, you got that?"

Intensity, paired with a strong denial of reality, really will carry you through.

ce

When I was in my early twenties, I worked at a bookstore. And since the universe likes a good laugh, I was awarded the self-help section. I think the people who come looking for self-help books are way too rooted in reality.

Shelving the self-help section helped me understand that there are a whole lot of problems out there—more than I ever thought possible. It's sort of like when I turned forty and needed to up my moisturizing routine. One trip down the beauty aisle at Target, and I found out my face has a lot more problems than I ever knew.

I spent the first few weeks in self-help reading my way through every possible bad thing we feel, think, or do. At the end of that month, I decided there should be self-help books for those who read too many self-help books. And yes, I realize, my book will probably be shelved in the same area of any bookstore, but remember, THIS book is the best and only self-help you will ever need. Or so the cats tell me.

One day a guy came in and just stood there, staring at all the books, while I carefully shelved the problems-with-food section. I learned to shelve quietly and stay out of the customers' way in self-help. I had the kind, whispery demeanor of a funeral director. I would lead my patrons to a certain section and silently pat them on the back and then fade away. But this guy did not want alone time. He wanted to talk.

"I need a book about anger," he told me, hands stuffed in his pockets and eyes scanning.

I grabbed *The Dance of Anger* (a great book, by the way), and we talked a bit about its message. He held it for a moment and then started scanning the shelves again.

"You got anything on, uh, worry?" He looked around, cagily. "Or . . . about relationships? I need something about relationships."

The guy was jonesing for self-help.

In my opinion, everyone should work the travel section of a bookstore for at least six months in his or her life—and never, ever work the self-help section. I made plans to hike in Costa Rica with a roommate when I worked the travel section. I discovered European backpacking books that made Europe a reality for me in the travel section, too.

And it was on those shelves that I found a book about small towns and their great diners, and I dreamed of road trips with endless cups of coffee and pie. I bought the book *The Best Small Towns in America* and randomly circled the name of a tiny Midwestern city because it sounded so adorable. Now, I live there. I had forgotten about that twenty-year-old notation until I found the book again this year. Serendipity. All from working the travel section.

If you can't work the travel section, then head over to entertainment and movies and dip into fantasy for a bit. Or go over to children's fiction and read *Stuart Little*. Don't be just a mouse in this life; be a mouse with a travel itinerary and a teeny-tiny red sports car. In sum, walk quickly past the self-help section. It's only going to beckon you with titles like *Feel Better RIGHT NOW!* or its sequel, *Not Feeling Better? What's Your Problem This Time?* Look away and head over to the children's section, which is remarkably less stressful. And there are beanbag chairs.

I realize what I am implying here is totally debatable. I guess I just remember too many customers in the self-help section seeming utterly miserable, and I think part of it was that they felt whatever was plaguing them had to go away, or get fixed, after ten chapters. We can't just be *in* the thing. We have to fix the thing.

Sometimes I am a lousy mom. And always, I am an alcoholic. I am *in* it. And yes, I totally think everyone should try for better and adjust their thinking and use all the tools they can to help make their lives the best they can be. That's a given. But what to do first? I think we need to sit with it: sit in the mess, embrace the fact that sometimes we are the star of a really crappy scene in life, smile, and say, "Hey. I am still here. And I am a DANCER. And I will dance my way through it, okay?" It's radical self-acceptance.

It's also a little bit nutty, but that's how I roll.

⌒

When I was a kid, my dad lectured me (a lot) about never doing anything "half-assed." Such a lovely term. And yes, I know this comes from the same guy who suggested that I have no expectations in my marriage, but I think he shifted gears on me when I reached a certain age.

Growing up, my dad ran a tight ship. He didn't earn the nickname General Patton for his lawn-mowing skills, folks. He liked order. And he abhorred anything half-assed. I remember one time being sent out to "go pick up sticks in the backyard," which was sort of like hearing "Bataan death march, backyard." After about ten minutes, my dad, who of course had been watching from the upstairs living room, was not pleased with my listless stick-picking-up technique. He marched over and showed me the minimum size of stick for picking, and then he demonstrated proper pickup procedure. I think he would have made me gather toothpicks out there if there had been any. To this day, I see a twig and I shudder.

But his point was that we need to do things right the first time. And I agree. I agree that we should do our best, work hard, break a sweat, give it our all, go for the gusto, and anything else that sounds like the Marines. This applies to things such as potty training our kids—when bodily fluids are involved, we really don't want to go halfway.

But then there's the scary stuff, including my big dreams, the inability to do Jedi mind control on my kids, and my first attempts at doing a crow pose in yoga. With those things, I embrace my inner half-assedness. I realize that sounds kind of like an awkward Kegel exercise, but I just do what I can. And whatever that is, I pair it with some flair, maybe some body paint, and a whole lot of enthusiasm. In my case, my half-assed attempt is covered up, but it's still the *Showgirls* system.

When my first book came out, I found myself plunked down in the strange and wonderful world of publicity. I loved my book; it was my third child. One small problem with marketing it, however, was my overwhelming shyness and introversion. I look at a group of people at, say, a Sunday-morning church service, and instead of seeing nice humans with Bibles and cute sweaters, I see a throng of talkative Middle-Earth marauders with torches and swords. It's an unfortunate thing to see people like this, especially when you hold up your precious book, hoping it will protect you—plus marauders don't tend to read much.

About two weeks after my book was published, I was late to a signing and was hustling down the sidewalk to the local coffee shop . . . when I fell. By "fell," I mean I did the splits. I suppose I could blame my shoes. They were strappy and red, and I wore them, along with red lipstick, to help me feel confident and sassy. That sass carried me right through a teensy patch of water, and then I watched as one foot slid forward and the other foot just stood there and did nothing to help. Cue the splits.

I guess it was time for me to add some razzle-dazzle to my book-signing game.

Post-splits, I tried to find my dignity, but it was all stretched out on the pavement. I didn't know who saw me, but I was on Main Street. It was three o'clock in the afternoon. A woman was doing splits on the sidewalk. It was kind of hard to unsee.

I got up, stood still for a minute, and slowly smoothed down my hair. Then, I responded the only way I knew how. I took a deep breath and said, "TA DAAAAA!" And then, I did jazz hands and pranced into my first book signing.

Embrace your half-ass.

To Half-Ass or No?

Things to Half-Ass

1. *Yoga.* Yoga classes are all about slow movement. I don't care how tiny and trim the women are in that sweaty, lavender-scented room; they are not watching you. They are trying to find their downward dog without falling over and killing it. Breathe; move slowly. Feel the half-ass.

2. *Casseroles.* As one who cooks for small children who hate anything not in nugget form, casseroles are the great mom shrug of the culinary arts. Take a protein, some frozen peas, something sticky, mix it up, and bake the crud out of it for thirty minutes. Voilà: half-ass cass!

3. *Dogs.* They need water, kibble, and a walk. And they think every breath you take is a magical vapor of holy goodness. Right now, a dog that has not left my side since 2015 is leaning on me. He worships me. It's easy love, and, of course, I don't deserve it. All I do is pat his head, and he quivers with joy. Codependent canine half-ass!

Things Not to Half-Ass

1. Brain surgery.

2. Driving a car.

3. Sobriety. But more on that in the next chapter.

CHAPTER THREE

HOW TO
be an alcoholic

Sometime after three years of recovery, Brian came home after work to find me slicing tomatoes with such drama that I could have shouted, "*Viva la revolución!*" with each knife flourish. He walked toward me and touched my shoulder. I tensed. Brian then kissed my cheek, and my cheek tensed. He complimented me on dinner. I narrowed my eyes. And then, Brian smiled at me and said, "Hi, honey. How was your day?"

That was the final straw. I declared war with Brian.

⌒

Most mornings before Brian leaves for work, I hand him his little lunchbox, kiss him goodbye, and sigh at how grown-up we are. Brian wears Dockers pants and has coffee and a black Thermos lunch bag that is sort of depressing, and before he opens the door he stares outside, takes a deep breath, and says, "Once more. Into the breach."

Brian heads off to a job that is sometimes not the happy land of wonderfulness and fulfillment that I would so love for it to be. I want Brian to be fulfilled in his work, like, *all* the time. This goes along with my general expectation that everyone in my family should be "living the dream" at all times. This type of thinking is sort of wired into my mom brain. I shoulder the hopes and dreams of all members of our household, including pets, because, well, *somebody* has to.

I turn around after he heads off into his breach, and then, I look at mine.

On this particular day, my breach is the kitchen. And I *hate* the kitchen.

My kids ate only two bowls of corn flakes and drank two small glasses of juice; however, my kitchen looked like it had been turned upside down and shaken. I couldn't really understand how two bowls and juice cups could be so destructive and mean.

Sometimes? Adulthood bites.

After an entire day of tackling kitchen counters, laundry, bathrooms, and so on, I started wondering, just a little bit, if I had any sort of purpose other than wiping things.

Later, I was making a healthy and delicious meal for my spawn when you-know-who had the audacity to return home from his breach. His job may not be all unicorns in Dockers pants, but at least he gets to drive in a car and go away.

Standing over the cutting board, I paused my chopping and found myself looking at my husband with a lot of anger. Like, a *lot*. It was all misguided and bent, like a ticked-off Leaning Tower of Pisa. Without realizing it, Brian became the seat of all things bad, mainly because he was coming in from the outside. "Away" was all I wanted to be at that moment.

"Away" sounded flipping wonderful.

This is not groundbreaking material. I'm not the first mom to feel like she plays a game called Monotony every day. I'm certainly not the first one to feel stressed or isolated after a day with two little kids. But, of course, I am an alcoholic in recovery, which makes things a little more interesting.

And no, I don't mean interesting as in TED Talk interesting. More like being stuck in the dentist's chair while he drills away, trying to distract myself by remembering all the lyrics to ABBA's "Fernando." That kind of interesting.

In my recovery circles, I learned the acronym HALT, which warns me not to get too Hungry, Angry, Lonely, or Tired. It is always good to have a reminder as to why you might suddenly feel unhinged. It might be that your children are feral. Or you just need a juice box. This is kind of tough to avoid because parenting makes you HALT all day long. A good part of my day as a mom is spent forgetting to eat or feeling alone or worn out. I would like to admit that I was never angry during those early parenting and recovery years, but that would be a lie. I felt angry plenty of times.

For example, I felt anger toward Brian for breathing over my salsa.

I stood in the kitchen with knife in hand, and I forgot my recovery. All of it. It was gone without even a wisp of recovery smoke to remind me. There was no earthshaking tragedy in my kitchen that fuzzed my memories. This was just a day, pretty much like any other, with salsa.

And it was taking me apart.

ᶜᵉ

Here's how recovery works—at least how it worked for me. I got sober, and it was wonderful and hard and life-changing and terrible, all at once. In the early weeks, I lived in this breathless treading of minutes, getting through Friday nights and long weekends and dinners out and kids, all without a glass of wine firmly tucked in my hand. There were times when I ached for the feel of that glass between my fingers. I swore I could sense it like some sort of phantom limb of addiction, fitting so smoothly and delicately between my fingers.

I once caught myself staring longingly at the glassware section in Walmart like I was looking at pictures of my ex-boyfriend's family.

For those first weeks, even brushing my teeth was a new discovery. No wine stains. No rumbling stomach and gagging. These were both good developments, but every little detail of my life was different and exhausting. I passed through the looking glass into recovery, and I was nowhere near as relaxed about it as Alice. Granted, my land of recovery was not nearly as trippy as Wonderland, thank goodness. Each day passed on with the same slow agony as I focused on getting through the next minute.

I realize this makes recovery sound awful, which is not really the goal, I assure you. But, sweet Jesus, those first few weeks were hard labor. They were physically and mentally demanding. They were Ironman tough, but without all the Speedos. Also, I had no knowledge of where the finish line was, or even whether there was a finish line at all.

On top of all this—as I was running the race all sweaty and exhausted—I kept thinking, "Maybe drinking wasn't so bad. Maybe I can drop out of this right here. Maybe . . . this whole thing is crazy." Pounding out the miles in recovery was hard enough without my evil anticoach in my head whispering in my ear that the whole race was pointless. "You should stop here," anticoach said. "You need to hydrate. Probably with an icy gin and tonic."

ᑎ

I wonder what it would be like if people in recovery were treated like Ironman athletes. I'm pretty sure early recovery is just about as harrowing. There are tears. And sweat. And agonized facial expressions. If I'm going to have to wear the tiny metaphorical Speedo here, I really would like to have a medal for it. And on the really tough days, I would like to wrap myself in one of those crinkly silver blankets you get at the finish line, creating a big, sober cocoon.

Of course, there would have to be the obligatory Australian commentator. I can imagine him speaking with his thick accent as I start my morning:

And Dana makes a rousing start from the bed into her morning routine without vomiting or wishing she were dead. And her entrance into making breakfast really shows us her strength, ladies and gentlemen! She really gives it a go! Look at that form as she wipes up three-day-old oatmeal, or what we hope is oatmeal, from the floor! Let's see how she handles the transition from basically waking up to parenting two small children. . . . Wow! Did you see that! She just powered through an entire shopping trip with her two boys in a cart that has only three working wheels! The mental strength alone while she kept her head at the whining-while-waiting-in-line stage is the mark of a true champion. I can't wait to see how the final leg, bedtime, carries out. Truly, a tough course today, but Dana is showing she has the will, by crikey!

Pairing recovery with an Australian commentator is not a bad move. It's rousing. On the difficult days, I want my own overly enthused narrator heralding my slow-motion dive into bed at 7:54 p.m. "Watch that again!" he would crow, as my head hits the pillow while I clutch not one but two books, an iPad, and an industrial-sized bag of Skittles to my chest. "She really has a smooth transition here from being a normal walking and talking human to total nighttime-cocoon mode with her silver blanket! Whatta ripper!"

There is just one problem. In recovery, there is no actual finish line. We might want one, but that's sobriety for you. We don't get to break the tape.

And lately my pacing has faltered.

⌒

My recovery started out with a strong entrance right into twelve-step meetings. I kept pace with counseling, journaling, and pushing myself through a rocky landscape. I kept up. I did the work. I thought of each day as a sort of prize, making it to my bed with the knowledge that I did not drink that day. That was enough.

And, after a few weeks and months, it did get easier. It always does. Once you do the work, the muscles strengthen, the head clears, and recovery starts to smooth out. Anyone who has trained long enough can tell you about the magic that occasionally happens while running, biking, or any other nutball thing meant to torment a body. Athletic types nod knowingly at this and call it "flow." After a while, the muscles rely on memory, the body responds, and you get to run with wings on your feet as you "flow" all over the place, which is better than it sounds.

This happened in my recovery too—until it didn't.

Recovery is not an event, a class, or a destination. In my case it was more like a complete shifting of life—taking all the parts and pieces of my world, turning them upside down, and shaking them a bit until all the broken bits hit the floor with a clatter. And then you repeat this until you die. Recovery also has the annoying tendency to be difficult to pin down with any sort of exactitude. I can't say, "I am at level-one sobriety. Should be going for my finals soon to see if I can pass on to level two. That's when I get to do an internship."

For three years, I did meetings and read and meditated and kept at it. I fed and watered my sobriety and was a solid, spot-on Super

Recovery Girl. I never considered that I would get tired, eventually, of all that healing. Getting better is hard work.

On the night of the salsa, I picked a fight with Brian because I was weary and feeling sorry for myself. That's no big news. But there was a third party involved, and it was my tired-out recovery. Third parties can really muck things up. I was sober three years at that point, and my days were not solely focused on not drinking anymore. That kind of desperation was long gone. I no longer fervently whispered the Serenity Prayer as I maneuvered myself through—minute by minute—giving the boys a bath and getting them into bed.

Now, there were many days when I forgot I was an alcoholic altogether.

Big mistake. Huge.

The fight with Brian was your basic, standard-model married couple fight. When two people sign on to be around each other all the time, they are going to annoy the heck out of each other at various points during their marriage for no reason they can reasonably ascertain. This makes marriage completely unpredictable and thus exciting.

"Whatcha making? That looks good," Brian asked. He totally missed my earlier icy rebuffs for two reasons: (1) He doesn't have that much of a mind for detail (it took him a year to remember my middle name); and (2) He is one of those annoying souls who feel like one person can "be silly and cheer the other person out of her gloom." This works on toddlers and puppies,* but it does not work on me. My reaction is to simply hunker down into misery with a nuance of rage.

And so, we argued about jalapeños.

---

* *Scratch that. Puppies are never gloomy.*

"I'm cutting jalapeños," I hissed.

"Wow! Jalapeños!" Brian stated, needing to make sure we were all on the same page.

"Yes, and they're SPICY, and I will put them IN THE SALSA because YOU like them."

Ignoring the large, angry, spicy-loving elephant in the room, Brian cheerily replied, "Well, that sounds yummy! When's dinner?"

"AS SOON AS I'M DONE MAKING AN ENTIRELY DIFFERENT MEAL THAT YOUR CHILDREN CAN EAT." I gestured with my knife at the offending peppers. "These . . . these will HURT our darling spawn. But you don't seem to CARE."

And Marital Spat #4,675, the Battle of the Jalapeños, continued on from there. There was the slander of cilantro, and Mexican food in general took a solid hit that night. When it was over, neither of us had a clue what the fight was about.

You see, I had forgotten I was an alcoholic; therefore, I had also forgotten what resentments can do.

Definition

Resentment: (noun) a state of being in which you find yourself furious about things that are sometimes simple but sometimes not. Sometimes resentment is legitimate, and sometimes it is not. And sometimes you should do something about it, but also . . . maybe not. In sum, resentment is wonky. But it can come at you, armed with a jalapeño, and take you out at the knees.

CHAPTER FOUR

HOW NOT TO
be an alcoholic

As I sat in my therapist's office, she looked at me with that pleasant, vanilla gaze of expectation that meant I needed to start spilling my guts. So, I took a breath.

"Last night I dreamt I was buttering toast. For, like, an hour."

There was a soft silence while she waited and then realized I was expecting her to say something. She lobbed a rather tired "oh" at me.

"Other people get to dream they are flying," I lamented.

Three years sober. That's a good thousand days without that slender glass in my hand. I'd managed all the firsts—the first sober Christmas, first sober wedding, first very sober date night with nothing to say to my husband, first sober scary movie. I'd done them all, multiple times at that point. It was becoming, dare I say, easy. Except for scary movies. I have decided that my life is just fine without zombies or mutant anything. Life is scary enough.

It wasn't a big deal, I thought, this whole alcoholic thing.

In the world of recovery there is an unwritten mantra: once an alcoholic, always an alcoholic. I can't unalcoholic myself. I had long ago passed one of those "Am I an Alcoholic?" online tests with flying colors, and so now the task at hand was to stay on the sober path. One day at a time. March to the beat. Stick to the straight and narrow. All these things involve walking, which is easy, right?

My problem was that I was getting a wee bit tired of just walking all over the place. I wanted glitz and glamour. Walking is so *pedestrian.*

Initially, in recovery, I was seeing Joan, my therapist, about once a month. However, it had been more like once every two months now because my schedule had been swamped. We caught up, but I kept eyeing the clock, wanting to make my time with her worth the money. And yet, there was nothing to talk about. I was good. The marriage was good. The children were still good. We were all walking along, the landscape was clean and simple and de-alcoholed, and I was bored out of my mind.

"The whole buttering-toast thing? It took, like, I don't know, an HOUR. And that was it. I buttered two slices of toast."

No response from Joan. Helpfully, I pantomimed a knife spreading butter.

"I can still hear the stupid knife scritch-scritching across it."

Silence from Joan. ·

"I don't even get to eat the toast," I complained.

Joan began doing the head tilt thing a little more. I wondered if she would get a neck ache from this. She tilted a lot for me, but she hadn't written anything down in her notebook the entire time I was there. Clearly, this toast material was lacking something. Had I run out of things to say? Did Joan and I need to break up?

There was silence. I looked around the room. Joan had a new Scentsy candle that smelled like a cupcake on steroids. I took a breath and searched for more.

"Oh! So, my husband and I had a fight the other night."

I noticed Joan visibly brighten, and I wondered how often the inner Joan deflated a little at the whole "please analyze my dream" thing. Was there ever a time when inner Joan thought, "Oh for God's sake, not the Muppets in the shower dream again. It's just too weird. Can we just call a spade a spade and decide this dream is totally nuts?"

I prattled on; she said very little, and I found myself again in that weird counseling place where I wondered if I was supposed to keep talking. Joan continued to tilt her head and stare—the Scentsy candle was more responsive. I felt like I was stuck at a four-way stop, and everyone was staring at each other. Joan was either incredibly patient or writing a grocery list in her head. I forged on.

"Yeah, it was horrible. I was mad about . . ." and then I sort of stutter-stopped because I realized I didn't have a glamorous description of what I was mad about. In fact, the whole "about" part was elusive, similar to trying to remember that one guy's name from that one movie you saw once. You know, the one with the dog?

"I don't know why I was mad. I was just mad. There were these jalapeños, and I hate jalapeños. Like, I really hate them."

I eyed her to make sure she understood how deeply I felt about jalapeños. She nodded.

I channeled my inner Eeyore and sighed heavily. "But I know Brian loves them, so I put the jalapeños in the salsa."

Joan's head tilted so much to its side that she looked like she was shaking water out of her ear.

I slumped a little on the sofa, and added, "It was silly."

"Please, Joan," I thought. "Just say something. Tell me it's not silly and that I need to book an emergency getaway spa vacation in the Caymans because I'm so horribly stressed. Tell me my husband is a jalapeño-eating piece of ——."

"How did Brian respond to you?" she finally asked. She seemed awfully interested in Brian. "Did he decide to engage in your . . ."—she gestured at me with wide circles and finished—"stuff?"

That word, *stuff,* is like summing up Sybil's multiple personality disorder by describing it as "a little glitchy."

I took a breath.

"He didn't at first, but then, after a while, there was yelling. He said I was overreacting. I told him he was a douche. It was typical married stuff."

Again, tilty head from Joan.

I mustered a weak smile. "I'm over it."

This is the deal with relationships. Rarely is any utilization of the phrase "I'm over it" actually the case.

ᕷ

I have a friend in Florida whose sole purpose in life is to post on Facebook those horrifying videos of sharks circling in the water that are actually yards away from unsuspecting swimmers. The water is blue and serene, and the little, happy dots that are the swimming humans continue being little, happy dots. All the while, black, toothy, shadowy things are coalescing and sending shout-outs for more toothy friends to join them—it's awful. I have to wonder whether watching these videos before making our summer plans would persuade us to never go swimming again.

That's also kind of how I feel about marriage. And recovery.

It's startling sometimes how similar they are. For example, marriage is long-term. At times, it can seem rather relentless. Marriage practically begs for the Serenity Prayer on a daily basis. True, I am not trying to detox from my husband, and he won't cause liver failure or lead me to make questionable choices when shopping online. I might need to detox from control issues tightly linked to my relationship with him, however. All of it is progress, and work, not perfection.

The thing is, when Brian and I got married, I kind of had it in my head that I was saving his sorry behind from a life of lonely bachelorhood. I was rescuing him. I had already helped him stop wearing a phone on his belt, and I managed that in less than two weeks. I could totally rehab the guy. I was *on* this marriage thing. I had a whole slew of *It's Marriage! It's Awesome!* books, Bible studies, and plans ready to go. We were going to be the best married couple in the world.

And so it went with recovery. I got the books, the studies, and all the plans, and voilà! I became Super Sobriety Girl.

Sobriety tells you the straight story. It sits you down and stares at you and says, "Kid, here's how it's all going to go down." And, if you really want this, you listen. But you have to *keep* listening.

So I created my sober playlist. I listened to others who were in recovery. I listened to books, podcasts, and blogs. I listened to my inner sponsor who told me to change people, places, and things. Also, I listened to my outer sponsor who said, repeatedly, "Dana, it is possible it's not all about you." I listened to music that made me happy and peaceful. I listened to my quads when they ached from running, and I listened to them thank me when I did the whole self-care thing and got a massage. And I tried not to listen to my husband's friend Neil who asked me, at a neighborhood barbecue, "What? REALLY? Come on, not even one?"

Or you do listen to Neil and then look him in the eyes and tell him *exactly* how you feel about even one.

I listened to the rules: lean in; go to meetings; don't drink in between. I continued to listen to my playlist when my brain started to sizzle and I forgot all my recovery tools and how to think anything but "My God. A glass of wine would FIX THE WORLD right now." I listened really hard then because that's a dangerous time for an alcoholic.

And I learned to listen even when that sizzle faded and became a soft hum way off in the background, like the Muzak at a department store while you're shopping. You might be all happy as you shop and are probably chattering away with your friends, but you still listen. Because as far away as that Muzak version of ABBA's "Fernando" might seem, it feels good to hum along. That is when you listen the hardest, when it seems the farthest away.

And then, somewhere along the road, I stopped listening.

I should have told someone.

I should have said, "Hey. The music is fading. How do you hear it, still, after all these years?" I should have asked for help. I was so good at asking for help at the beginning, but I didn't want to ask the same questions again. I was afraid I would be docked points for repeating myself. So, I kept on treading water.

When my kids were in swim lessons, one of their instructors totally freaked them out one morning by barking, "Right! Okay! Kids, today we're going to learn how to drown!" My children stood shivering at the side of the pool, skinny arms clutched to their chests, eyes wide. The instructor just barked, "Everybody in the pool!" It was quite an opener, but as my boys bobbed in the water, teeth chattering, the instructor explained: the first instinct of any swimmer when he starts to struggle is to struggle harder. This is totally human nature, but it is wasted energy that only makes him sink sooner. One of the best things for a swimmer to do when he starts to tire out is to simply stop moving and float, arms spread out wide. Then, renewed, he can swim again.

"On your backs! Stick your stomachs up!" he bellowed to the class. "Now, relax! Just breathe! Let the water hold you!" There was a wet kerfuffle of arms and legs, and then I watched as my boys, blue-lipped and buoyant, stared up at the early-morning sky. Their scrawny white chests rose and fell with each breath, and they floated, smiling in the sun.

I had forgotten how to float. I had forgotten that letting the water hold me up was a possibility. And I had forgotten that, in my recovery, just treading water would kill me.

And all the while the sharks had started networking and were slowly approaching.

Tools to Help
Jazz Up Your Recovery

1. Wonder Woman footie pajamas. Also, spend ridiculous amount of time googling "Superman cat costumes" because every Super Sobriety Girl needs a sidekick.

2. Limited edition, artisanal, craft sodas that have ingredients like lavender and rhubarb. They have to be ordered from upstate New York, and the email newsletter you receive from the company is headed with something like "Hey, Dana."

3. Google "hot actors who are sober."

4. Goat yoga.

5. Google "hot sober actors doing goat yoga."

6. A tattoo of the Promises of AA on your lower back. All sixteen sentences of it. So, maybe your upper *and* lower back. With a butterfly.

7. An entire "Sober [Your Name]" audience button on your Netflix queue. Now you can answer when asked, "Who's watching?" *Sober* you, that's who.

CHAPTER FIVE

HOW TO

relapse

IN

footie pajamas

Christmas morning had arrived. I was in our bedroom, clumsily pulling on my husband's present: footie pajamas with some bizarre purple space monkey motif, including a hood with small, rounded ears. I turned around to see the tail, and just kept turning, because that's what happens when you discover you have a tail and you're an idiot. I slowly zipped up and caught a glance in the mirror.

I was ridiculous. And I was buzzed with enough vodka in my system to make my floppy ears bearable.

No one else, not even my husband, had any clue I was drinking again. I started the night before Christmas, and over three years of solid recovery blazed up like a Christmas tree afire. I was in trouble.

I admit I didn't want to write this chapter. I would rather have cleaned out the vegetable crisper drawer. I even offered to cut my cat's toenails, but he turned me down. Quite adamantly. But as I look back objectively, the relapse was probably the best thing that ever happened for my recovery.

Three years earlier, sobriety had taken a tired, wrinkled, sick version of me, grabbed hold of my hand, and said, "Hey. Come over here with me. Sit down. Let me get you a La Croix. And let's talk." And it was glorious.

Except when it wasn't. Which was often. At times, it was about as fun as getting physical therapy for my sciatica when I was pregnant. This undertaking was not glorious. It made me squirm in pain and sort of woozy afterward, and yet I had to go or I wouldn't be able to walk or give birth, both things that I was kind of locked into at the time.

Some days, recovery left me sore and wobbly. These feelings were totally fine and normal, not to mention being all about acceptance and being a grown-up. But somewhere along the way, I filed away a resentment about getting sober. It was tiny and often smushed down by realistic, grown-up thinking, but it was there, living in the basement of my mind.

I thought my sober story should include daily unicorns: fabulous ones, *real* ones, ones that walk up to you in the middle of paying a parking ticket and shake their mane, saying, "Girrrl. You are SOBER! You don't have to pay that ticket. Let's sashay over here and go shopping!"

I do realize this thinking is total crap. Life can be crap: children get sick and puke all over you, your Visa cards get stolen, and your husband can make that sound he does when he eats. And, because of all the sober chocolate you are shoveling down, you grow out of your skinny jeans. I dealt with all this daily crapola by using the tools I had in place. They helped keep Sober Dana's engine purring throughout all this, smoothly through all the hills and valleys.

But I forgot that the tools only work when you decide to pick them up.

And all the while, that unicorn hung out on the couch in my basement, waiting to make his grand entrance.

I stopped going to meetings around the holidays. By "holidays" I mean the great trinity: Halloween, Thanksgiving, and Christmas. In early October, I found myself in that happy zone when *It's the Great Pumpkin, Charlie Brown* started showing up on the airwaves. I was aflutter. The air was crisp and scented with pumpkin spice. And somewhere in there, mixed in with the homemade astronaut costumes, the pumpkin patches, and all the leaves to rake, I stopped going to meetings.

Cue the scary music.

This is the part where the big-eyed girl goes into the creepy house and asks, "Is anybody there?" Then she proceeds to walk right up the stairs.

This is the part where I should have listened. It's the part where I should have turned around and run the hell out of there and into some meetings.

When I dropped one tool, I didn't decide to let all the other ones fall to the ground. But it's similar to my "healthy" eating history. The days that I decided to eat a Super Fudgy Nut Bar for breakfast were usually the days that I had more Super Fudgy Nut Bars for lunch, which meant no salad in my future. It was only Super Fudgy Nut Bars. *All the time*. That's when I would end up licking chocolate crumbs off my T-shirt at dusk as I watched an infomercial about food dehydrators that can steam clean my floors.

Fall ended. I raked all the leaves away and continued right on into Christmas. This blessed holiday, as you know, is what divides the strong moms from the weak. If there ever was a hill I was going to die on, it was Jesus's birthday. This is really so not what he wants for his birthday, but I had started to feel guilty. There were no tangible guilt-making events that were in play here, just a floating sense of "I'm screwing up" that kept scratching at me. And nothing fixes guilt like an absolutely perfect Christmas.

Meanwhile, the unicorn in the basement was practicing his Christmas carols.

Tools were dropping to the ground all over the place. I had misplaced my Big Book. The morning devotionals were replaced by sleeping late, and my Serenity Prayer had been archived. As these things dwindled, my anxiety grew—the addict's teeter-totter.

I finally attended a meeting. I managed to wedge one in between Christmas shopping and heading home. My friend Keith—who is a dead ringer for Ernest Hemingway with a silver beard and grizzled manner—greeted me with "Where have you been? I've been worried about you" and gave me his viselike hug. I explained about all the church events, choir concerts, and caroling parties. He just looked at me and gripped my hand with his rough palm. Keith is officially an old-timer. He takes no crap. He loves me, and I felt his blue eyes bore into me as I rattled on. He was quiet, though, offering no warnings, no advice.

The thing is, recovery is more than a metaphorical bag of tools that you schlep through life, one day at a time. It's a heart issue. I had all the help I needed right in front of me. You can lead an alcoholic horse to water, but you can't make him drink. Or not drink, I guess, depending on how you look at it.

My heart had gone cold.

ↄ

I once lost a precious earring: a tiny, dangly emerald that was misplaced somewhere in the mess of our bedroom. My husband had bought the pair for me way before kids—when we had disposable income and could afford romance in the form of precious, teeny-tiny gemstones. Lost things really annoy me, most often to the point of obsession. I need to find the lost item because if I don't, I am a slob. I have been trying to convince myself this is not the case since I had two children. Unfortunately, slobdom and children are total besties.

My stare swiveled around the room, and I vowed to find the earring because then, just once, I would be leading on the scoreboard: Mom 1, Slobdom 0.

Twenty minutes later I was covered in cat fur, digging out the detritus underneath our ancient radiator. I found seventeen cents, forty Legos, three marbles, a golf ball, and something that looked like a sock but was so covered in grey fuzz I couldn't tell. The pile sat before me, and I unfolded myself from the floor. One of the cats gleefully batted a marble across the room, and his footsteps stirred up poofs of grey fluff as he walked. I sighed.

"I know you're in here somewhere," I growled. "It's only a matter of time, earring."

I became a bit . . . unhinged. And all I had to show for it was a furry sock and some change.

My Christmas unfolded in a similar fashion: me looking around frantically amongst the piles of wrapping paper and cookie sprinkles and hoping to find that one precious thing that would make it all better. And all the while, all I kept coming up with was dust.

Three hundred yards of twinkle lights couldn't answer a soul that was sick. But they were so sparkly. I was just like my cats, willing to bat the glittery bits around for a while until I was exhausted.

About three days before Christmas, I stood in my kitchen, listening to one of my twelve Pandora Christmas stations—one station for every mood. As I stared at a menu for Christmas Eve, I thought, "All this needs is a nice glass of champagne."

Now, let's be clear. This thought has occurred to me 157,980 times before. As an alcoholic, celebration drinking is difficult to let go. It's understandable. It's one of the last vestiges of drinking done right. Happiness and alcohol, actually together in the same room, had not been a thing with me at the end of my drinking days. I was a warm-vodka-out-of-a–plastic-bottle kind of girl at the end. But there had been days, long ago, when drinking happened because of just fun and happy things. When I quit drinking, picturing that golden, slender glass of delicate bubbles because a fun, happy thing was occurring nearly brought frustrated tears to my eyes. But it got better. Sobriety trumps fizzy alcohol anytime.

That's what recovery teaches us. And recovery is super smart and right, every time. Sober is Harvard University taking a look at your SAT scores, but still being nice about it. Before, when those itchy feelings of a drink would bubble to the surface of my brain, I would listen to recovery, and it would throw a few slogans my way, such as "Think through the drink," or "Sober is bettah," like my sober Boston buddy tells me. Or "What the hell is wrong with you? DRINKING IS NO LONGER AN OPTION, YOU NINNY." Okay, that's not a slogan that you would see printed and thumbtacked to a wall in my meetings, but it still works well.

But this time, I guess Burl Ives and his holly jolly-ness drowned out that voice.

No, that's total crap. Burl Ives was not at fault. He's Burl Ives. Nothing is ever Frosty's fault.

We are all built with an inner compass, and that inner compass is what directs us while watching our children sleep, eating kale, and watching videos of corgi puppies. However, it doesn't push us;

it simply points. And in my kitchen on that cold winter morning, I came to a decision.

I was going to drink again.

Just over the holidays, though.

Because if I kept drinking, right on to Groundhog Day, that's when I would have a problem.

But who doesn't drink on New Year's Eve, really?

(Sober people, for one. Sober people don't drink on New Year's Eve. And also me, for the past four years.)

Then my vision became tunneled, and I tilted my chin a bit in that stubborn way I've done ever since I was little. And the planning started.

Picture the briefing room at the White House before invading some bad country. That's not even close to the workload involved here. Initially, I had to work on PR because this was not a relapse. It was a perfectly planned "break." If I had had a bullet journal back then, I would have scheduled my "break" in tidy calligraphy.

I didn't actually start drinking until Christmas Eve. Waiting those extra days only further proved that this was not a problem. I was simply taking a vacation from sobriety for a short while.

The trip to the liquor store was interesting, but I was on autopilot by this point, so I wasn't really checking whether something interested me or not. I stuck to the plan.

I stood in front the wine display and waited for all the bottles to lean forward and say, "Hey! Old friend! It's so totally okay that you're doing this because we know you're just on a planned 'break'! And look! Your favorite German wine with the super long name is on sale!"

"*Ja! Guten Tag!*" said the German wine. The Italians just stared.

I stared back at all the pretty bottles and waited for something like a blip of happiness to drip down into my heart, delivered via a wine IV.

No spark of glee glistened back at me in those display cases. No inner Kevin Bacon shouted, "Let's paaaaarty!" while I stood there. I looked around, searching for some fabulous new peppermint-flavored chardonnay for me to try, but no such luck. So, I grabbed my Gewürztraminer and then wandered through the mazes of bottles to the reds.

I was going to get one bottle of red, and most of it would be used in my spaghetti sauce. This, of course, really played well in my "this is not crazy" plan. Red wine after nearly four years of hard-won sobriety wasn't crazy; it was *culinary*. I picked up a bottle.

After my stroll through the aisles, I headed to the checkout and made polite, "this is not batshit crazy, this is a break" small talk with the checker. I didn't have any sort of major tremors or panic. I just coolly pulled out my credit card and discussed red sauce and holiday plans and whether prosecco is better than champagne. Somehow, in my mind, since I had decided I was taking a "break" from sobriety and doing all of this so rationally, with only two bottles in tow, I proved my point.

I had this all under control.

And I had lost my mind. But that was all under control, too. Because that's how people who are going crazy on a nuclear level think.

I plunked the bag down into the passenger seat, and that's when the bottles started clinking. It was then that I made the shocking realization that I had wine in the car, and I was going to *drive it home*. For a moment, I wondered how I had made it out of the shop without lights or sirens or at least one of the salespeople pointing at me and screaming like those pod people in *Invasion of the Body Snatchers*. Don't they have a list of alcoholics up by the register like they do with all the stolen-credit-card people?

Even in my drinking days, I always had problems with liquor stores. Walking through their doors always made me feel uncomfortable because I felt at any moment someone would see me come back out, laden with bags of wine, and shout, "Unclean!"

Perhaps it could have been that inner compass of mine, tugging at my sleeve and reminding me, "Alcoholism is plague-ish with your family, Dana. Let's go get a McFlurry." Also, I always wanted to look at ease amongst bottles and bottles of things I didn't ever really feel old enough to understand. If there had been a section labeled "Don't worry! This wine goes with everything," I would have been thrilled. I attended a wine tasting once at a winery in Bordeaux, France, and all I remember is thinking, "Why do they keep giving us these teensy cups to drink out of? I don't need to note the color. I just want to drink it, not paint with it."

Those clinking bottles took me right back to when I used to drive home after stopping to buy wine with both my boys in the backseat. I would sing "Thomas the Train" and joke with them as we headed home, the car and my spirits buoyed by the pact that the wine had made with me. The bottles would roll and clink and say to me, "We will make you feel whole and shiny and brilliant upon opening. We promise."

We know how that all ended.

It was the clinking that reminded me.

I remembered looking into the rearview mirror and my boys' brown eyes searching out mine. I remembered promises of *Little Einsteins* DVDs, ice cream, and endless other loopholes, so we could all survive life together for the next few hours because Mommy was slowly fading away into nothing.

I could have pulled over and thrown the bottles out. Instead, I reached over, tucked the brown paper more tightly around them, swaddled and safe, and continued home.

I didn't drink the bottles for two more days. It was easy. I could wait. And on Christmas Eve, when I finally did crack open a bottle of red, I made sure it was all very according to plan: one glass for me, one glass for the red sauce.

It would be fitting to tell you that the first sip was horrible. I wish I could tell you that. I can't even tell you it was wonderful. But I can't really remember the taste at all. I know I stared at the wine, sitting quietly in the glass, and I wondered at it all. How could a liquid substance be so . . . *pushy*? Think about it; army generals and mothers have the power to slam us around, bark orders, and make us storm the beaches under their direction. But a liquid? Inanimate and sloshy? Why fear it?

And so, I drank it—because it's not the boss of me. There was no gorgeous "ahhh" that I wanted. I mean, if I'm going to do this, I deserve to really enjoy it, right? But instead, nothing. No big "Wow, that was awesome" imprint. I remember thinking the wine smelled very bitter. But perhaps that was just my soul, folding its arms and giving up.

Sometimes, God has a really vicious sense of humor. I'm told all the time we forget childbirth so that we'll do it again. But I *remember* childbirth. There was a lot of heaving and hoeing and noises and fluids. I yelled at a lot of people. I do remember it all, extremely well, thank you very much.

I also clearly remember that my husband thought it would be funny to buy me footie pajamas. And that Christmas morning, as I opened them, hoping for the adorable sock monkey flannel pajamas I had spotted at Target and mentioned to him twice—once in a text with pictures—I felt somehow the purple-and-brown space monkey tragedy was a perfect fit.

But I don't remember the taste of that wine. I try to conjure it up, as a sort of forbidden gift, but there is nothing.

Somewhere between the night I started drinking again and New Year's Eve, I returned to the liquor store, bypassing all the sophisticated chitchat about red sauce and entertaining, and bought myself a large plastic bottle of cheap vodka. This I kept in my old hiding place: my closet. As I shoved it down amongst my boots and clothes, I remember a sharp *thwap* in my brain that said, "SEE? DO YOU SEE WHAT'S HAPPENING HERE?"

Also, I remember on New Year's Eve day, my little boy, Henry, figured it all out.

Henry was just about four at the time, and the whole figuring-out thing happened in an unglamorous, yet fitting, way: sweet Henry was sitting on the toilet. Henry loved his toilet time, much like his father. He liked to hang out in there, sing a little "Bob the Builder," and ponder the meaning of life. Henry did not like to rush bodily functions, and I was fine with this because it meant containment. I knew where he was and what he was doing, and unless there was some sort of level-red, hazmat kind of situation going on in the loo, it was a break for us both.

I left Henry to do his business and poured myself a lovely vodka and vodka with a twist of vodka. I made sure to put it in a normal glass, probably something plastic with a superhero on it. Although I missed using barware, I never attempted to use wine goblets or a rocks glass with this whole trip to Insanityville.

As I walked into the bathroom, drink in hand, I was at that slightly off, humming stage of early evening where things were not sloppy. Mom just seemed like she'd hung a vacancy sign above her head.

And then Henry, sitting on the toilet, stared at me and said, "That's your special drink, isn't it?"

Afterward, he smiled, but his smile was the uncomfortable, tilted kind that he gives me before we visit the doctor, trying to convince himself he's not afraid. "Is there gonna be a shot?" Half smile. "I'm okay with it. I just wanna know. So will there?"

There are moments in a parent's life that we don't forget. We aren't allowed. They are filed away, framed perfectly, and they resurface when we pray, or are drifting off to sleep. It was his smile. It broke my heart.

Henry never saw me pour the stuff into glasses. He didn't see the bottles. To the best of my memory, all of that had been successfully contained while they were watching endless *Little Einsteins* or playing in the train room. I never poured a drink when the boys were in the kitchen with me. And, four years ago, when I first got sober, Henry was barely a year old. But somehow, he knew.

And he looked afraid.

I drank a lot that night. It was New Year's Eve, after all.

Some More Pithy Recovery Sayings That Totally Apply Here

1. You're only as sick as your secrets.

2. If you are coasting, that probably means you are going downhill.

3. Drinking again will send you right back to where you left off: Crazy Town.

CHAPTER SIX

HOW TO

master

THE

ugly cry

Do you know why they recite pithy sayings in recovery meetings? Because they're true.

And who's the "they" behind the sayings? A bunch of people who know Crazy Town all too well. They have visited it personally and have the pictures to prove it.

I was one sad space monkey.

On New Year's Eve, I tried to make a fantastic dinner because we were parents of small children, so dinner at home and a movie was really all we were going for that night. New Year's Eve always has such pressure to be super exciting. If we start out the new year with a boring meal that has to include chicken nuggets and *Veggie Tales*, then we might as well start researching minivans.

So, I was busy making all sorts of sexy *amuse-bouches*—otherwise known as food my children make gagging noises at—and stirring up all sorts of vodka in orange juice for me. I wouldn't be eating much, since the vodka seemed to provide all the nutrients I needed at the time. I was going off plan on this night because Brian was already home; the prior nights, I finished any sort of drinking before he showed up. But I was getting braver. It seemed the more orange juice concoctions I stirred up that evening the braver I became.

Again, this is when my brain should have given me another resounding *thwap* and said, "BRAVERY-SHMAVERY. YOU JUST DRANK VODKA OUT OF A *VEGGIE TALES* GLASS."

But my alcoholism had shoved a sock in my brain, tied it up, and put it in the closet, which is a weird analogy but that's really how it felt. There was more room in the closet because the warm bottle of vodka had moved down to the kitchen because I was tired of endlessly climbing stairs for refills. I hid it behind the flour containers. I figured Brian wasn't going to bake anytime soon, so I was safe.

There wasn't much more to say about that New Year's Eve. It had a high-pitched, amped-up hilarity—provided by me—because this was going to be the best New Year's Eve! Ever! My husband provided a sort of puzzled amiability while my children picked at the adult crappy food, drank Sprite out of plastic champagne glasses, and hopped right onto the kiddie ride that I had created for them. But still, the evening had a frantic feel like the exhausted, sticky end of the night at a carnival's closing time.

At one point I considered putting some of my special drink in a plastic champagne glass. I missed the actual glasses in which I could put a drink—the slender, delicate stem of a wine glass balanced so prettily between my fingers, like a conductor's baton. A heavy, manly crystal rocks glass felt like a heavy weapon, ready to throw at someone at a moment's notice, if need be. When I used to drink the manly brown stuff that I poured into those rock glasses, their weight tethered me and kept me from wafting away altogether. Then there was the impossible and tippy martini glass. It made me feel like I was on an episode of *Mad Men*, until I spilled it, which I always did. And how could I forget the champagne flute, which makes any drink into its own decoration?

However, I did not put the special orange drink in a plastic champagne glass. At least I did one intelligent thing that night. Doing so would have resulted in me being more careful with my intake because that glass could have had the chance of being mixed in with the other glasses sitting around; therefore, I might have not gotten as totally blitzed drunk as I did. All this led to the ugly version of Dana showing up in a much shorter amount of time than anticipated.

Of course, the ugly version of Dana was not part of the plan. But show up she did, somewhere in between the main course and our fancy flan-thing for dessert that no one liked because it was rubbery and tasted like sweet eggs—drunken baking wins again.

I started to get that uneasy and fractionalized realization that I was not okay.

There are levels of inebriation in alcoholism. We have the gentle, glowy inebriation that we long for, that we would write love letters to if we could, because it is so elusive for us. There is also the frenetic, super energized inebriation that makes all sorts of household chores super easy. If the cat boxes are in their worst state or your husband gets trapped under a car, this is the most opportune level.

Then there is sleepy inebriation that results in . . . sleeping. You don't even get to enjoy the inebriation. You're passed out on the couch with your drool, and hopefully no one takes a picture.

There's also angry inebriation that is pretty awful and ugly, and no one ever thinks that will happen. No one starts out with a couple of margaritas thinking, "Well, in about an hour and a half I'm going to alienate all my friends on social media and probably reduce my children to tears. Cheers!"

The angry inebriation level is often paired with total humiliation inebriation. Total humiliation inebriation is often difficult to remember. So that's a plus.

However, the level that I had reached on New Year's Eve was past all of that.

In one of my trips from the kitchen into the living room, where all the frivolity was, I realized the floor was not in a straight line. And my thinking started sliding off into immobile nuttiness wherein my brain was zipping from thought to thought in a frantic search for some sort of sanity, but my body was not able to keep up. So, I plunked myself down on the couch in the hope that no one would notice.

And no one did.

This makes a lot of sense because rarely is my family paying attention when there is television involved. We were watching something kid-oriented and cute, and all three family members were now slack-jawed and focused. I could have ripped off my shirt and waved it around my head at this point and maybe, just maybe, Brian would have looked up and asked, "Are you hot, honey? Should I turn the heat down?"

I would have thought that making it this far without detection would have made me happy, but I had bypassed logical; that's if you call relapse and manipulation and clandestine behavior logical. It's alcoholic logical, I guess.

So, I was past all that. I was about as messed up as one can get while being in a living room, not in some hospital somewhere. I found myself sitting dejectedly on the spinning couch and feeling sorry for myself as Brian took the boys up to bed. I had lucked out with missing the bedtime routine; Brian volunteered, and I certainly didn't want to give kisses and hugs in my state. But I felt so alone as I sat on my couch. I actually felt sad that no one noticed I was doing something so very wrong. In the teaching world, we learn that the kids who misbehave are usually the ones who are longing for the most attention and love.

I, in my sad space monkey pajamas, had really acted out. And yet, no one had noticed. I had no threats of expulsion. I didn't even merit a detention slip.

And this made me even more despondent.

So, I started to cry.

It was the kind of crying that has no other description except that it was phlegmy and wet, and my face turned red, and I made noises like a dying baby seal.

At last, my husband noticed. He came down the stairs and did that head-tilty thing he does when he's trying to process information, which kind of makes him look like a school counselor.

I took a gulp and reached out to hold down the couch, and then I whispered to my husband, "I drank. I'm sorry."

He answered, brilliantly, "What? You drank what?" And he actually looked around for the cup as though I had ingested some cleaning spray by accident, or because I was really that stupid.

I stared at him, rather stupidly, because vodka produces that look a lot. I was really *that* stupid.

And I said, slowly, "I'm drunk. I drank. I've been drinking."

I sounded like an inebriated French lesson in verb tenses.

And my poor husband stared at me some more. If I had had better vision at this point, I could have watched his face travel through a variety of expressions, starting at incredulity, moving to anger, and landing at disgust. Brian, who had been so understanding and compassionate when I first got sober, had no ability to conjure up those feelings on this night.

Maybe, just maybe, while I was adding more and more vodka to my orange juice during my relapse, I wanted someone to find me out.

Maybe I wanted my husband to discover me, mid-pour, and knock the bottle away, all dramatic and terminal. Maybe I wanted someone to take my drinking from me instead of me having to hand it over by confessing.

Maybe I wanted someone to put a stop to this whole mess sooner. But it doesn't matter. I probably wouldn't have listened. Recovery always has to be my choice. Addiction doesn't like to listen to others. So, I made my misery and then I sat right down in it for a spell, all wretched and alone. All the while, I was shooing away anyone who had the audacity to suggest, "Hey, you look kind of awful. Are you all right?"

So, here was the best news from that night: I finally said, "I'm not all right." And, once again, I stopped.

My Relapse
Gratitude List

1. I am grateful I didn't get the keys and get in the car while I was drinking.

2. I am grateful I didn't start that car and start driving, in search of more wine.

3. I am grateful I didn't have my children in that car.

4. I am grateful I didn't get pulled over, doing a breathalyzer outside my work, my church, or my kids' school.

5. I am grateful I didn't kill someone.

6. I am grateful I didn't kill myself.

7. I am grateful I looked into the abyss of me.

8. I am grateful I can say, "But I'm still here."

9. I am grateful for the memory of it, even the horror and the pain. Even the sadness.

10. I am grateful for all of it.

CHAPTER SEVEN

HOW TO
deal
WITH RELENTLESS
disappointment

I t's a Wednesday night, three days after the space monkey relapse and reveal. I'm up in my bedroom, frantically pawing through my lingerie drawer, which seems to contain nothing but lingerie. I start to panic. This was where I stashed all my sobriety chips, tangled in with all the satiny, stringy things, but they were nowhere to be found. Don't ask me why I chose to store these precious things amongst my sexywear. I guess I figured they'd never see the light of day, and so they'd be safe. But now, they were missing.

In my twelve-step program, all anniversaries, from the first twenty-four hours onward, are awarded with a small, round medallion that looks like a poker chip, only fancier. Initially, I did find some irony in this comparison. I was all "I dunno, punk, do I feel lucky?" with staying sober, and the whole thing felt like a risky gamble.

As I continued to search among the lacy undergarments, I did find a thong that had "I ♥ You" emblazoned in very uncomfortable rhinestones across the crotch. It was from my long-ago honeymoon, and it was still in the drawer; however, my sobriety chips were not.

I found my chips later that week while I was helping my boys clean out their playroom. We were sorting small plastic toys from other smaller plastic toys, and then I heard it—a familiar jingle of metal. My son, Henry, was sitting in front of a small treasure chest, and inside was a pile of plastic tokens evidently stolen from Jumpin' Joes, the local fun center/child casino. Also, there were my chips. All of them. I didn't know where to place most of my malaise: on the stolen coins or the fact that my boys had been rifling through my underpants.

At my next meeting, I decided I would return my chips. I wanted to come clean and start over. It seemed like the best gesture to help with this. It was a healthy thing to do, all honest and redemptive. And, as is often the way with virtuous stuff, I kinda felt sick to my stomach about it. This dread was heavy and real and ran in tandem with the gloom in my heart about starting my sober walk all over. I do realize giving the chips back is not the whole story. Recovery doesn't have a total reset button; it keeps growing even when we falter. Yet I was having a hard time remembering that. I couldn't see the recovery forest for the disappointed trees.

Recovery is hard. Recovery, part two, is harder. It felt all repetitious and tedious and fraught with gloomy "What in the world was I thinking?" kinds of feelings. It felt second best. It felt just like *Grease 2*, in fact, only without the singing and dancing. Sometimes you should just stick with the original.

I shoved the chips in my pockets and clinked my way into a meeting. As I walked down the long hallway to room 202, the chips seemed to weigh an impossible amount. My sadness and I would have made a really unfortunate entrance if my sagging shorts had dropped down to my ankles as the door swung open. "Hi," I would sigh. "I relapsed. And now, I can't wear pants. I'm a mess."

My pants stayed on, and I made it in the door. I was greeted with the usual chorus of "Dana! Good to see you!" and waited for the inevitable questions: "Where have you *been*?" or "You look *awful*. Do you *feel* awful? DO YOU HAVE SOMETHING HORRIBLE TO TELL US?"

No one said anything like that. There were smiles and hugs, and the whole time I had a weird grin plastered on my face and felt like I was Milli Vanilli, preparing for my press conference. I felt like a big, fat fraud.

The first meeting I attended when I initially got sober terrified me. I sat in a badly decorated room with those weird slogans on the walls, staring at my shoes. I was so uncomfortable and afraid.

The first guy to speak at that meeting had a spider web tattoo on his skull. Just looking at it made me want to find him a hat. But as he started talking in his soft drawl, I was a goner. This man *was* me. I could be the girl with the spider tattoo. And it all made sense; I was home. And we all lived happily ever after. Or so I wished.

Now, I was back at home, feeling like I had robbed the place.

As my friends spoke and worked their way around the circle, all I could focus on was how many people were left before it was my turn to speak. I had turned into that kid who hates reading aloud in class and can only concentrate on when he's next. I had tunnel vision and barely listened to the stories. I certainly didn't have anything to share about that night's topic. I was mired in me.

Four speakers away, I contemplated having a sneezing attack and leaving for a tissue.

Three away, I figured a bathroom break would work. I was feeling pretty queasy.

Two away, the lady's story was so completely nutball tragic that I got sidetracked and did find myself listening. It involved something that sounded like it was straight out of the movie *Roadhouse,* which, if you don't know, involves Patrick Swayze and a mullet. That kind of stuff just can't be ignored.

One down. Totally time to just make a break for it and run.

And then, it was my turn.

"Hi, I'm Dana. And I am, most definitely, an alcoholic."

When one of my boys tells on the other, his sense of detail is always elaborate if not accurate. There is a lot of gesturing, adverbs, and long, windy sentences that would make Tolstoy proud.

"And then," Henry would begin, flinging his arms out toward me like Frankenstein's monster, "THEN, Charlie TOOK THE TRUCK AWAY." Next, his hands would wave up and down as he continued, "And, I said, very NICELY, 'Don't do that, Charlie. I would prefer that you not do that right now.' VERY NICELY I SAID THIS TO HIM." This is paired with some vehement head nodding and waggling of eyebrows like a mini Groucho Marx who had turned informant. "And Charlie? He just WALKED AWAY AND LEFTED ME ALL ALONE." His right hand would point off to the horizon, and he would place his left hand on his forehead. And all during Henry's explanation, I would wonder where I could start auditioning him; he could make us some money.

However, when we tell on ourselves, the drama factor is vastly reduced.

"I messed up," I confessed as I stared at my hands. "And I really didn't want to come here tonight." I took a breath and forced myself to look around the room at their faces. "This is harder than . . . well, this is the hardest. This is just the hardest. Telling you."

Telling my husband had been easy compared to this. I love my husband. But he is a normie, and his ideas about alcoholism and recovery are still at the Little Golden Book level. He just doesn't get it.

When I first got sober I used to really hate his lack of understanding, thinking that marriage meant he had to be with me in the trenches, gutting it out with me every step of the sober way. But as time passed and I attended more meetings, I started to realize that asking a nonaddict person to feel all my feelings would be about as possible as socking him in the stomach to help him understand labor pains, which sounds kind of fun but ultimately is not a good plan for building empathy.

Besides, if anyone ever tells you that marriage means sharing everything because you two are so connected, that's just bullshit.

My friends at the meeting sat for a moment, holding their Styrofoam cups and making a lot of healthy eye contact. That's their thing. And these are *my people*. These were the beloved weirdos who had sat with me for years in countless meetings, drinking the same horrifying coffee and sharing my life when they told their stories. They had walked me through it from the beginning, offering constant encouragement and listening, and I had totally let them down.

To my right, Gerry spoke. "First of all, you have not let any of us down."

I had somehow made it through my story without ugly sobbing or a bathroom break. In meetings, cross talk, or directly addressing someone else's story, is often discouraged. It's not group therapy in the sense that advice is batted around like a Wiffle ball, aiming at specific incidents or tragedies to heal. Cross talk is something newcomers all think will occur because I believe that's the only way we can wrap our minds around what a twelve-step meeting is. We talk, and then they talk about what we just said, and it's all about us. However, the truth of a meeting is spoken one person at a time, with only his or her message. Healing happens as we hear ourselves in those stories. And here's the coolest part: I always hear myself in the voices of the others sitting around that table. Always. And every time, my heart unlocks a little more. What is more powerful than realizing that the guy with the spider web tattoo and a few less teeth than you is your twin? It works.

So, I was surprised when the meeting goers, one after the other, talked right to me.

"You didn't let us down."

"You are so brave for speaking up."

"You came back. Good for you for coming back. Not all do."

"Just keep going forward."

"We are so proud of you."

I nodded and smiled with tears in my eyes and my love for this group rising in my chest like a great big bubble of gooey feelings. This. Exactly this. This was what I needed to hear.

And then, Jim spoke.

"Well. I, for one, don't really know what in the hell you were thinking. You need to pull your head out of your ass."

Well.

Jim had been attending meetings since the 1800s. He was what I like to think of as "crusty." Not in the literal sense, because that would be kind of gross and a possible medical issue. Up until now, Jim had been a beloved fixture in our group, telling his stories and often detailing his gruff gratitude for the steps and his sobriety. He was a grumpy old codger, yes, but harmless. I like to think of him as Grumpy Lite, like the beer, but nonalcoholic.

Until this meeting.

In this meeting, Jim took me down like napalm.

Jim proceeded to talk for about five minutes about my failure to take the message seriously and my lack of gratitude. Five minutes is a really long time when you are being scolded up, down, and sideways. I kept thinking Jim might be finished when I heard a long, rather raspy pause, but it seemed he was only taking a breath, gathering more oxygen into his codgery lungs for the next onslaught.

I believe a proper term for all of this is "dressing down." It made sense because by the time Jim was done with me, you could hear the last indelicate "pfffffffffft" from my sober balloon, and I was a sad little pile of wet rubber, lying on the floor.

It was awkward.

I had not considered this detail in my taking-a-break-from-sobriety plan.

Sometimes, we go crazy. Britney Spears shaved her head. Sinéad O'Connor ripped that picture of the pope. Mel Gibson behaved horribly on the phone, and *Entertainment Tonight* was more than willing to broadcast it for all to listen in. In my small corner of the world, I had come back from crazy, and crazy does not sit quietly. In other words, if a crazy tree falls in the forest, you better believe people are going to hear about it.

It's what you do after the crazy that matters. Not so many people hear about that. It's not as loud or interesting or photo-worthy after all.

When I came back from my relapse, I felt like I had just walked out of a darkened movie theater, blinking at the light after a weeklong horror show. However, as much as the world seemed garish and bright, I'd take it—no need to start liking scary movies now. But still, at times it was a crap sandwich. And Jim was part of that.

It's official. I was no longer Super Sobriety Girl.

Thinking back to New Year's Day, my family had plans to go to a pancake feed at our church, and as much as I disliked the idea of going, with a pounding head and so much despair, I forced myself to go. Brian was barely speaking to me. My children were pretty oblivious. I *was* a horror show. But as I sat and managed my way around some carbs and syrup, I looked around. Our church was a group of people whom

I loved. And I knew they loved me. If I had decided at that moment to get up on a chair and announce to the whole group, "Hello, my name is Dana, and guess what? I AM A WALKING CRAP SANDWICH," they would have surrounded me with prayers and hugs.

That was one message I received after this whole mess. You matter. You are loved. No matter what. All is grace.

Jim's message differed: You matter. Listen harder. You are loved. No matter what. And the truth really hurts sometimes.

And I needed to hear them both.

It hurt to relinquish my super sobriety cape. I hung it up, right next to the space monkey pajamas, and sat with that hurt for a while. I had forgotten the whole sitting-still part of recovery. "Have a Holly, Jolly Christmas" had been on endless repeat in the background of my life for so long, and that's so *not* a sitting-still song. But, thankfully, Christmas was done, and New Year's was over, and Valentine's season didn't have quite the social press, so I sat.

If I were the type to write a holiday letter, that year's would have been a doozy.

Hi, folks! Wishing you well from our sweet little town. Brian is doing great, I think. Maybe. Not really sure, actually, because I just assume he's doing great, and we haven't had a real conversation since October.

The boys are also doing great. They seem clueless about a lot of things, and that is so a plus right now. I am all about clueless children at this point. But in general, I'm sure they're all super smart and super gifted and all, I guess. But really, this letter is all about me, so let's move on.

So, lately? I kind of lost my mind and then found it, and here I am. Some would say I'm a shell of a woman, but I don't think so. In fact, I think the nugget of the real Dana is finally here, unshelled and a little loco, waiting to get her skin back on and live.

That sounds all sort of creepy and like that no-skin lady from *Hellraiser*, and nobody wants that in a Christmas letter, so God bless and Merry Christmas. I'll hopefully be able to have a real conversation with a number of you in the near future. For real. Like, I mean, if you actually tried to talk to me right now, I might sort of stare at you or break into tears. So don't call me for a while; I'm on sabbatical.

So, in sum, we're doing all right. We're actually doing fine. Finally. And how are you?

And it is a Happy New Year, considering.

Sincerely,

Dana

I could blame the baby Jesus and his really packed social calendar for my relapse. I could blame the glossy holiday *Better House than Yours* magazine covers and too much to do while surrounded by sticky little kids. I could go back and blame the genes thing, but I covered that in my first book. I could blame my husband, but he gets so much crap from me anyhow.

After all is said and done, I can tell you a list of reasons why I relapsed. But, really, I am not exactly sure. All I know is that something clicked or a knob got turned to a different setting, and then there I was, hiding vodka in the stupid closet again.

I relapsed because I'm an alcoholic. That's all.

Not all of us do, but if you're lucky enough to come back from one, you better make it count. Or there might not be any more whack-job Christmas letters to mail out in the future.

New Year's Resolutions
from Here On

1. Be kind to yourself.

2. Be kind to others.

3. This includes pets, husbands, and people who drive
   slowly in the left lane.

4. The end.

CHAPTER EIGHT

HOW TO
live a rich
AND
fulfilling life

Long ago, in my early thirties, I decided to stop waiting for a husband to show up who would travel with me on vacations. This was a slot in my life that had not yet been filled because for some reason I had decided that traveling to a *fun* place solely for *fun* reasons entailed a male escort. That didn't sound quite right, but you know what I mean.

Anyway, I got tired of waiting for my world to open up through the bliss that is marriage, and I booked my own darn vacation. This was the real deal. Choosing my adventure involved hours of internet research, and this was before TripAdvisor existed. The destination I chose also meant a pretty solid price tag, but I saw *City Slickers* in my twenties, so I was all in.

I booked a week at a dude ranch. It had been nearly twenty years since I had been on a horse, but it seemed so romantic. The big mountains. The big horses. The big blue skies. All the big things.

When one books a trip to a dude ranch in Wyoming, amongst horses, mountains, and real, actual dudes, it is extremely important to have the right cowboy hat. So, of course, I ordered mine online from Urban Outfitters.

The hat came in the mail about a week before my trip, and I placed it carefully on my head and analyzed my level of "dude" in the mirror. It was a slouchy-brimmed monstrosity that would have looked perfect on Dwight Yoakam, or perhaps one of those *Coyote Ugly* girls. It was huge and slipped down over my ears. I seemed to have ordered the "extra-large hat oozing coolness."

No matter how the hat fit, it was an essential part of my trip. I shoved it in my suitcase and hoped it wouldn't end up flattened because that would mean the coolness had sprung a leak. I thought of it as a lid that kept the contents inside and thus proved that those contents fit in the world around it.

So, I zipped up my suitcase and left on a plane to Wyoming. As I flew over the mountains as wide and high as God's footprints, I hugged my arms tight to my chest. Dude ranches were for families. They were for romantic getaways. They were, maybe, for groups of men who wanted to fly-fish and do other rugged things. When I felt the plane dip under the clouds and start its descent, I started to wonder whether maybe, just maybe, dude ranches were not for a single woman in her mid-thirties. I started to wonder if perhaps I might look a little bit silly.

The first morning there, I pulled on jeans, cowboy boots, and a flannel shirt. I looked in the mirror and took a deep breath and pulled the hat down over my ears. I felt ridiculous. And then, as I walked down to the stables to meet up with the other guests, a wiry fellow fell in step beside me. He was about my height, and the best word I can use to describe him is *dusty*. He too had a hat and boots and looked like he had been born that way, boots on and all, unfortunately for his mama. I smiled at him nervously, trying to look like my whole outfit was not brand-new. I wanted so badly to give the impression that I simply sauntered through things in my life. In fact, I didn't want to just saunter; I wanted to walk like this cowboy at my side.

I wanted to *amble.*

I wanted to wear a cowboy hat and not look like I was posing for a tintype photo at a souvenir shop in Branson. This was the story of my extreme, painful, and totally out-of-proportion self-aware story: I was SO self-aware that it seemed like my environment was constantly pinging up against me like judgmental sonar. I was a self-aware submarine of neuroses, and putting on a cowboy hat only accessorized them.

The cowboy at my side made twangy small talk. He asked me where I was from and whom I was with, and I told him I was from the Midwest and single. He broke stride for a moment, glanced at me, and asked, "You're here by yourself?" This would be the first of the twenty or more times this question would be lobbed at me during the trip, to which I would always reply with the fascinating answer of "Yes."

As we all met down by the corral, I managed to hoist myself up onto the fencing without hurting anything. I perched there—all calm and cool—like sitting on fence posts was totally what I did all the time back home. Then, the dusty cowboy looked up at me and said, "That's quite a hat you have there. You gotta extra-large head?"

Up until then, I had actually liked Mr. Hat Expert Cowboy Dude. No longer. He was dead to me.

The dude ranch experience ended up being an exhilarating trip. All week I rode a Paint Horse with the stunningly accurate name of Bucky. Bucky had a rather delicate disposition, it seemed, which manifested in a strong distaste for getting his hooves wet; therefore, he would gather himself and spring over each creek crossing— something Mr. Hat Expert Cowboy Dude failed to warn me about on our first ride. The thing with Wyoming is that a large number of its creeks are really creeky, and the landscape consists of craggy rocks and cliffs, so pretty much any time that I got onto Bucky I was praying for dear life.

As the week progressed, I learned to love Bucky and all his springing about. I loved Wyoming with its big skies (Montana stole the tagline) and rocky mountains high (popularized by John Denver) and really tall cowboys (minus my short antifriend cowboy). I ate great meals and made some good friends that I swore I would keep in touch with forever and then never saw or talked to again. It was awesome.

One night the ranch hands—I'm not sure that's the right term for the men and women who worked there, but we're going to stick with it because it makes the story have a more rugged appeal—invited the guests out to a honky-tonk in the nearby town of Cody.

I was all over this. For one, I was still single; therefore, I figured all the single cowboys at this place would surely congregate around me like flies with little cowboy hats. Just to clarify here: I was the honey. Also, there would be alcohol. At this point, I had not yet figured out that booze and I needed to break up, so I was more than happy to go have some drinks.

Unfortunately, the drink on tap was beer. I don't know why I was surprised, given that Cody was all outdoorsy with no frills, so brown liquids would be the main inebriate. So, I ordered a Bud Light and grimaced through it. I'm not a fan of beer. I realize this is a somewhat goofy-sounding thing for an alcoholic to say, but that's only because the common perception is that we alcoholics lurch about like liquor-slavering zombies, looking for any sort of cocktail to gnaw on. Not true, at least at the beginning. We can carry on with our alcoholism for years while holding on to our wine goblets and tippy martini glasses. The more often we can label/camouflage our drinking with phrases such as "Napa Lover," "Wine Enthusiast," or "Mom's Special Juice" the better.

Anyway, the honky-tonk was fantastic. It was packed tightly with cowboys and loud, twangy music, and how we managed to find a table was a small miracle. I waited with Clara, one of the Swedish cooks. (This means she was from Sweden, not a chef of lutefisk and those wretched meatballs.) The men brought us some beer and Clara said thank you in her adorable lispy accent. Clara had that whole gorgeous Swedish babe thing going, if you're into that. We both sipped our beers and did the usual look-around, although I think I did so with a lot more anticipation. Clara seemed rather tired, and I imagined her blue eyes and honey-colored hair had collected more suitors than my fly-to-honey analogy ever could. I didn't mind so much. Clara was quiet and nice, and I was glad to have a sister-in-arms. But after a while, I began to notice that no cowboys were approaching our table. I know this because I was still sitting, and all the other folks were standing around the bar. It's simple math.

I felt a bit deflated. I had on lipstick after all. I had expectations.

It was then that my life took a wonderful turn. I refer to this historical event as "When Carl Danced with Me."

Carl was a guide and rancher at the dude ranch. I have changed his name, incidentally, because to reveal his name would give away that this man actually exists, for real, in Wyoming, like *right now*. No sane woman would remain anywhere else. They would pack up and go looking for Carl, and that's just not good for the survival of our species. Anyway, Carl had arrived a bit later than our group, and I had yet to meet him. He ambled in, escorting his lovely and hilarious wife, Carla, whose name I also made up. I know I could do better here regarding names, but she just looks like a Carla. She had silvery-white hair that was braided into pigtails, and she made red neckerchiefs work. She had a whole "let me go out and kill a chicken and then make you a pot pie and some peach cobbler" vibe. She was earthy and funny, and I kind of wanted her to adopt me, which would have been rather weird because I also wanted her husband, Carl, to marry me.

Carl looked exactly like Sam Shepard if Sam Shepard was hotter. He had silver hair and a fantastic mustache that could have had its own Twitter handle. He was tall; he took up doorways. He wore slender, dark-blue jeans and a plaid western shirt. He just oozed wholesome hard work, and I'm talking the sexy kind. I never understood the whole "he's a tall drink of water" thing until I met Carl. He is so wondrous he could be his own water park destination.

So, in sum, Carl was delicious. And then, he asked me to dance. And lo, Carl could dance too.

Carla seemed not to mind, by the way. I think perhaps she was used to this. Perhaps Carl was paid extra to entertain the womenfolk at this ranch, which I realize now sounds really creepy, but Carl doesn't do creepy. He does honorable and good and all things right in the world, and as it turns out, Carl has some serious honky-tonk moves. Carl dipped and turned me so many times I became dizzy and giggly like that doe-eyed girl who tangos with Al Pacino in *Scent of a Woman*.

That dance was over ten years ago, and I remember it with cinematic clarity. In fact, I often revisit that moment when I am irritated with my husband. It's nice to throw my inner Carl at Brian when he farts on me in his sleep. "Carl doesn't fart," I mutter as I stalk around our bedroom, opening windows and shooting Febreze in Brian's direction. "Carl smells of cedar, and baby birds alight on his shoulder as he walks."

It's possible I have put Carl on a bit of a pedestal here. Carl deserves it. He is so wonderful.

Having a vivid imagination had always been a skill of mine. But in my postrelapse days, I let my imagination slip into a sort of "Secret Life of Walter Mitty" existence. I daydreamed. I stared off into long distances. I tried to conjure up Carl with so much regularity that he deserved his own Hallmark Channel. Not only did I pine for Carl, but I also longed for that Wyoming girl to come back. I missed her. She was young and fun, and she could drink a glass of wine, or four, and dance with tall cowboys all night long. Now, my life was dishes and laundry and children, and I found myself slipping into fantasy and not dealing with reality well at all.

But maybe reality is not all we imagine it to be.

The first time I got sober, I was lucky enough to experience what a lot of those in recovery refer to as "the pink cloud." This experience, which sounds like a very chichi drink, is a period in the early days of recovery where the haze and mire of addiction lifts, and elation follows. I believe, in retrospect, that just walking and breathing after the toxins have left our bloodstream feels like we're walking on clouds. We're high on life. Literally.

In those early weeks of recovery, I found myself driving home one night from a meeting, and I burst into tears. These were the happy kind of tears; the ones that flowed simply because the sun was setting, the sky turned a warm coral, and Gerry Rafferty's "Baker Street" just came on the radio—in other words, heaven. I had to pull over. As I sat there, weeping and allowing the saxophone riff to heal my soul, I figured I could not get more pink-cloudy than this.

But, lo, I did. The following days were filled with these almost religious experiences that involved me doing everyday things. I went on walks and looked at more clouds, sometimes doing both at the same time without walking into a tree. I hugged a tree. I hugged my children. I ate an apple. I hugged my children after feeding them apples. You get the idea. I was in my own bliss blitzkrieg. It was a practical mixture of my body finally feeling better and my Higher Power giving me huge high fives for getting sober.

What a lovely experience.

Also, what a short experience.

The great Christian theologian C. S. Lewis described conversion as initially a spiritual exhilaration. But then, eventually, God sets you down and expects you to walk. Things can't stay perfect and floaty forever, otherwise it's not a worthy relationship. It's the same with recovery. After a while reality sets in, and real life lumbers in with it. The next time you try to give your kid a hug, he reaches up around your neck with his sweet, pudgy little hands, and you notice the reek of poop. Upon horrified, slow-motion investigation, you realize that it is all over his hands because he's a toddler, and he investigated the poop. (To those of you who think, "Oh, that never actually happens in parenting, right?"—it does. And sometimes more than once in a month's time. Think potty training. And if that isn't the best way to truly comprehend responsible birth control, I don't know what is.)

During my Dana Gets Sober, Part Two, experience, I did not get the pink cloud. I didn't even get a burnt-orange cloud. This sucked. My days were long, and my recovery seemed nothing but a tedious slog through redoing everything I had already *done*. After all, I had small children. They open their eyes in the morning and ask themselves, "How often can I make my mom repeat stuff until she snaps?" I was being bludgeoned with the redo, and it was all so exhausting.

I kept waiting for that spiritual energy to arrive, swooping in to save the day and letting me know that yes, I could be Super Sobriety

Girl again. The pink cloud and I could become a sort of superhero team, solving crimes and buying gourmet coffee for my home group. But I would demote myself to sidekick this time. I could accept that. Since this was my second go-around, I would allow myself to step down into the Robin role because I was humbled.

Instead? I had days where the most interesting part of my twenty-four hours was taking a hot shower. I was not energized. I slumped a lot. If anyone even asked me, "Paper or plastic?" I would start crying at having to make a decision. I felt, often, that my Higher Power was watching me, arms crossed, in an omnipotent "Mmm-hmm? You gonna listen now?" kind of way.

I know this makes my Higher Power sound really mean, which he is not. My Higher Power is Jesus, after all, and Jesus doesn't really do mean. He doesn't say, "Well, neener-neener, Dana. I TOLD YOU, didn't I?" and flounce off like a mean girl.

But he did, I think, let me do relapse all on my own. I'm sure there were a whole lot of reasons for this, outlined in some great Higher Power file in the sky labeled "Dana—Tough Love." One day, when I get really smart or die, I will get my answers. For now, I will go with the command that my dad used to bark at me about yard work: "Dana! Do it right the first time!" So, let's review: recovery should never be done half-assed.

The thing is, I have a loosey-goosey take on reality. I liked that my existence needed to be draped with a lot of daydreaming, romantic expectations, and soaring soundtracks. For crying out loud, I'm a teacher who lives in the Midwest; what else am I going to do?

My mom told me a story once about her mother-in-law that describes this inclination toward dreaminess. Mary was a farmer's wife. She had what we like to think of as "grit," also known as "She's a total badass but also a little bit bonkers." She worked achingly hard her whole life and then said, "Wait, I'm not done," and went off to scrub a floor afterward.

She said things such as "Well, daggone" whenever she saw us. We still don't really know what that means, but that word had grit, too. Mary didn't have a lot of time for romantic comedies on television or daydreaming. Daydreaming was what Dorothy did in *The Wizard of Oz,* and look what happened to her.

Enter Julie, my mom. I don't think *grit* when I think of Julie. Actually, that's not true. She has been married to my dad for over fifty years, and the two of them should earn a true grit medal for this miracle. But Julie is a woman of Beethoven, flower arrangements, and Hepburn-and-Tracy movies. She likes to write long letters and has a total love for all the *Anne of Green Gables* books. I am thinking Mary didn't read much. She was too busy butchering hogs.

Julie recounted talking with Mary one afternoon, and Mary eyed her and said, "Well. You're kind of a fairy-tale type of person, aren't you?"

I'm thinking Mary might not have meant that as a compliment.

Julie and I are kindred spirits in the whole fairy-tale thing. Granted, with age and wisdom, she has put aside some of the whimsy. Marriage, tragedy, or parenting will do that to you.

For the record, my mom is so not an alcoholic. I think I remember her telling me that alcohol to her just sort of "tasted bad" and some other nonsense. When pressed, she said she'd order an Irish coffee once in a great while, but mainly that was because of the whipped cream. I find this weird. Alcohol that has the extra step of scraping off a topping, and is scalding hot? That's just too much work.

But I get the fairy-tale thing. I so often love to hunker down in my head instead of in the cold, hard world. I think a lot of alcoholics do. And, I mean, why not? Did I not just say the world is cold and hard? Do you remember 2017? Just, like, *the entire year* of 2017? Need I say more?

Julie reminds me that life has magic moments, and if I can't find any, then I need to simply orchestrate some of my own. This gives me strength on the days when I have to clean the bathrooms, and the futility of such an act nearly makes me sob because I am surrounded by small boys with really bad aim. Reality, shmeality. Why is this so bad? I mean, unless I'm talking to the electrical outlets, or leaving my family to begin my career as fire-baton twirler for the Moscow Circus, we're good. Fairy tales are just stories. I love stories! And as far as I'm concerned, living happily ever after, at least in my head, is not totally bonkers. It's creative. Yes, I am convinced. Everybody needs a Julie.

ↄ

When I returned from my dude ranch adventure, I was more than happy to relate to my friends and family how I had been rugged and outdoorsy for an entire week, and survived. I rode a horse up the side of a mountain at such an angle that the ride began to take on a sort of funhouse tilt that terrified me and irritated the horse. I saw a moose. Up close. He seemed grumpy about it. I shot rapids. I drank whiskey and learned to tie my own fly lures and my behind got saddle-sore, and I was proud of it. I conquered the West, surrounded by real cowboys, real horses, and a really big sky.

A week later, I received an email from my ranch. They were excited to share that the ranch had been selected for a photo shoot for a little-known publication called the *Sports Illustrated* Swimsuit Edition. Some raw shots had been sent as part of the newsletter. In one photo, a blonde woman was leaning back over a hay bale, wearing something about as substantial as two pieces of twine and some hope. The whole thing made me smirk. This was about as fake as it gets. But then I looked closer, noting her cowboy hat.

Mine was way cooler.

My Super-Duper Scientific
Spectrum of Reality

Good & Real
———
I'm not sure.
Sobriety

Good Fairy Tale
———
Carl
Hallmark
Christmas
movies

Bad & Real
———
Shark week
Mortgages
Doctor visits

Bad Fairy Tale
———
Hansel &
Gretel
The Bachelor

CHAPTER NINE

HOW TO

recover

FROM

being human

S etting: Therapist's office sometime in my thirties, or what I refer to as my "in-between time." I remember I sat on a large leather armchair that made awkward farting noises every time I moved. Thus, most of the hour occurred with me trying to remain perfectly still. And this pretty much sums up the whole appointment.

"So, can I have a hug?"

My therapist was the one asking, and it wasn't a good kind of hug, and it hadn't been a good kind of therapy. I tried to extricate myself from the chair without sounding like I needed Pepto-Bismol.

"No!" I blurted with more emphasis than I think either of us expected. I hoped Mr. Creepy Therapist Guy made a note of my newly acquired assertiveness because I still wanted to gain imaginary therapy points, even though his request was completely inappropriate.

Mr. Creepy Therapist Guy looked disappointed. "Well, we talked quite a bit about how you don't like physical touch from men," he continued. "So, I was thinking we could hug and that could be a start on getting better."

Yes, he really did say that.

And that was our first, and last, appointment together.

Mr. Creepy Therapist Guy might still be working somewhere, but not with me. During the entire hour, he had questioned me at length about sex, and things went from uncomfortable to smarmy in about ten minutes. But something happens when you sit in that overstuffed leather chair, and you see the certificates on the wall: you keep talking. You just keep talking.

"Well, I had a relationship that didn't go well. And he left me. And since then, I guess, I haven't really trusted anyone."

"And what about your physical relationships with men after this?"

I looked around the room as if to find an answer that fit how I was feeling. I wanted to say, "It's so much more than that question. There is always so much more to it than just sex. Sex is only a bit of string I have tied around the huge bundle of mess that I am carrying around with me. Sex keeps the mess tidy—at least for now. And would you stop asking me about it with that look on your face?"

I don't remember what I actually said to him. It was probably some of the truth and some not. So much of my life during my in-between time followed this script, a balancing act between reality and my own fiction.

Reality was so overrated in my world back then. Still is. But once I embraced sobriety, I was able to embrace the magic and the truth of my existence. Back then, fictional living only occurred because it was for survival. Fairy tales, under duress, are not nearly as fun.

My therapy session had not been fun. As I left the office and walked past the reception area, I glanced at the woman at the front desk. She looked up at me and said in a low voice, "Are you scheduling another appointment?" And I shook my head no. Maybe it was my imagination, but she didn't look surprised.

I have thought about Mr. Creepy Therapist Guy a lot since our session. A toxic relationship with a man who I thought would be my husband had ended, sending me into a tailspin of depression and despair. As a result, I had found my faith, but I still had so much pain, hurt, and messiness to deal with. I was in between. My thirties felt like I was standing on an empty road, looking back at burning ruins. Ahead, there was only a long, empty road. I had Jesus with me, though, so I figured I would walk that road for a bit, hand in hand with him, and then at some point he would smile knowingly and hand me off to my future husband and I would be so happy. Because that's how Jesus works. He's like eHarmony, only less expensive. With him, I would find love, healing, and, perhaps, a rainbow.

Instead, I spent about eight years single, wandering and often drinking a little too much. I may have gotten out of a bad relationship with a man, but I was beginning one with alcohol. So, I was between a drinking life and a sober one, but I didn't know that then.

I wonder about the therapist. Is he still practicing? Was he legitimately creepy, or if I was so messed up, did he even have a chance? He sticks with me. Creepy things tend to do that.

crↄ

I have been in therapy since my middle twenties. And I kind of hate it. Mr. Creepy Therapist Guy became my one big reason why I don't like to get counseling; however, there are a few other reasons to add to the list.

I hate therapy because it costs a lot of money. I hate going and talking to someone, and it costs me as much as a new pair of shoes. Shoes are not talkative, and they do make me feel better, nearly 100 percent of the time. Therapy is kind of a crapshoot. Often it makes me feel queasy, and shoes—even the really tall ones—never do that.

And I hate it because therapy doesn't offer much in tangibilities. I don't get a certificate stating, "Congratulations! You're so totally sane!"

Therapy is lonely. It isn't really something I can talk about over a latte. It makes me feel naked, and nobody really wants that in a coffeehouse. I certainly can't post about it on the internet, which is what most of us do about everything. So, no Instagram posts with me walking out of the office all tear streaked and soggy, clutching forty sodden tissues and stating, "Went to therapy today! Doc says I need to journal about rage and abandonment! Time for a smoothie!"

I also hate therapy because it really hurts.

Therapy tends to scrape out stuff that has been firmly lodged in your insides for far too long. This image is both gross and disturbing and completely fits how it feels. It's a dentist visit for your soul, and I hate it.

As much as I try to avoid it, I hate that therapy keeps showing up in my life, like an awkward suitor asking me to date him. I want to tell him, "It's not you, it's me, Therapy," but in this case that's really true, and I can't deal.

Basically, I hate therapy because it loves reality. And you know how I feel about that stuff.

ᑒ

When I was little I used to have horrible nightmares. These dreams were the kind that would make a great scary movie today, if the director were on acid. The worst dreams were the recurring ones I would experience with a kind of bored horror: "Oh, this again, but yes, I'm still terrified." The most memorable nightmare by far was where my mom completely disappeared from our household, until I discovered that she had been sucked under the refrigerator. She was still alive, and, as I recall, she seemed rather embarrassed about it all. But still, she was under there. We all had to live with knowing my mom was under the fridge for the rest of her life; there was nothing we could do. If that dream doesn't pretty much sum up domesticity on a daily basis, I don't know what does.

I do realize that dream sounds pretty ineffectual, but I promise, it was horrific. And yes, trying to relate a scary nightmare often comes across as rather meh—"Oh my gosh! I have to tell you about my dream! My cat stole my Visa card, and I thought he ran up a three-hundred-dollar bill for cat toys at Target! Except it wasn't TARGET! It was Macy's!"

Looking back, the refrigerator dream doesn't make me shudder at all. It just makes me feel sorry for my mom. But I had that dream for over three years, and I think the truly horrifying part here is that it had the audacity to keep showing up.

My relapse felt like that dream: sort of embarrassing, even nonsensical, but so horrible. I began to realize that I would always be working on myself. Like, forever.

Cue the scary music. And cue the therapy appointments.

I live in a world of extremes. It's more interesting that way. So, it's easy to say Mr. Creepy Therapist Guy is proof that I never need to set foot in another counseling office. It's so much more interesting to swing on that pendulum of all-or-nothing. Dana Gets Sober, Part Two, was starting to learn that life is all about forever living in the middle— and persevering anyway.

I know. Cue the *really* scary music.

A few days after the relapse was when the forever-ness really settled in, and not so pleasantly. My husband and I had a fight. In the history of marriage, fights are pretty common, and we have them regularly enough. When done right, they are a way to clear out the plumbing and air some feelings that need an extra whoosh of oxygen to be revealed. A marriage that is bereft of the occasional argument is weird and plastic.

But sometimes fights can be done very badly.

Did you ever watch one of those train-wreck brawls on reality television, where the idiocy is at level ten but the ability to put lucid thoughts and words together is at zero? Think that, but without alcohol and the spray tans. It kind of makes our fight sound worse because booze at least gives you the excuse for incoherency.

Brian and I had been circling each other since I let him know about the drinking. Actually, I had not really let him know about the drinkING, just that I drank, and then I got very, very quiet about providing him with any more details. I figured if he was interested, he would ask.

He didn't ask. I remember every so often making eye contact with him—as you do when you are married and occasionally have to say, "Please pass the salt"—and I would quickly look away. One part of me longed to sob in his arms and unload as if I were on my own episode of *The Jerry Springer Show*. The other part wanted to skulk away and become very, very busy and thus invisible. And all of it was barely held together by a strong sense of dread.

This whole wanting/not wanting thing is something I struggle with. I want attention, and then I cringe at compliments. I long for communication and then run away when it gets real. I figure this all goes along with my Nutball Pendulum of Despair. For the love of God, it's very dizzy up here.

I finally had it with Brian's silence, so I picked a super brilliant time to talk about it—while Brian was watching playoff football. He was leaning in toward the television, intensely chewing on some popcorn, and I sat down next to him on the sofa and began.

"I am sorry I screwed up. I am sorry I'm such a total mess. I am just so . . . very . . . sorry."

To his credit, Brian had actually muted the game and was facing me as I said this. But when the tears started, I think I actually saw Brian's inner Brian roll his eyes. Outer Brian would never do this because he is generally kind and pretty patient, and rolling your eyes at me is a way to lose your eyes. But he seemed to sigh a little, so I pounced.

"What? Am I being too dramatic for you?"

And you know what? This time, I think I actually was.

And you know what else? Brian was really *mad*.

Like, all of a sudden, he was really, really mad. And we were off to the races.

"You don't even seem to care if I am sober or not." I poked my fingers at his head with angry emphasis. "Are you even in there?"

Brian swatted my hand away. "Yep, I'm here, Dana. Taking care of our kids. And our house. And working. I'm HERE. Why weren't you?"

"I DON'T KNOW. I just know I feel alone, and you can do super dad and super worker, but what about super husband? I haven't seen HIM in a while!"

"PROBABLY BECAUSE HE'S TIRED OF YOUR CRAP."

We stood, staring at each other. I was preparing for a certain-death comeback because that's usually my thing. I am good with words, and so I know the zingers. And this fight had long ago taken a turn into not wanting to work out anything at all. All it wanted was to hunker down and lob as much of the arsenal at the enemy as possible in hopes of total annihilation. We were out for blood.

And so, that's when Brian decided to win the war. He stood up from the couch and turned to me and thundered, "YOU HAD IT ALL. YOU HAD ALL OF US HERE WITH YOU. *AND YOU PISSED IT ALL AWAY.*"

Then, he stalked out of the room.

Brian had been angry with me before. We're married; we've had some really intense fights about all sorts of fun things that married people fight about. All those arguments came down to hurt feelings, which stemmed from the fact that we really did, deep down, love each other. And we would get back to that loving part, eventually. It might take a day or two, but we always did.

But this time, it felt different. When he left the room, I felt it. A part of him, maybe just a small part, had chipped apart and fallen away from the marriage. Lost, maybe forever.

I sat on the couch and stared at my hands and felt the great heave of sadness inside me develop into more tears. They filled my hands and my lap and seemed to fill up the room. I was awash in misery, and he wasn't going to save me. Neither, right then, could I.

I asked him about this fight much later, when the relapse was on the long-ago horizon and we had picked up as many pieces of ourselves as we could find to put back together. Marriage means the pieces are not only yours or his. There are also parts that connect the two of you, like puzzles tethered. We were lucky. We found most of those bits, and we carefully set them in place and continued. And when I asked him about that fight, whether he might have left me, whether he was done, he looked surprised.

"I would never leave. I'm married to you, for better or for worse. It was a lot more worse at that point, but we're good now." This is Brian's kind of answer. It is a whole-picture kind of thing. It is simple. It is often very heartening. Yet, I wonder.

I still wonder whether Brian left himself, a little. He left his ideals, I think. The knight, the one on the white horse who saves the day, was defeated. His wife had one-upped him in the battle, and he didn't even know he was in one. And I think he hated me then, a little. And for Brian, hate hurts. It's his kryptonite.

Relationships would be so much easier if they didn't involve relating so much.

When I was drinking, alcohol had a funny way of stopping up my ears. I couldn't hear others around me, nor could I hear myself. When I stopped drinking, my ears could hear, and I could listen. Hearing *and* listening do have to work together, it seems. So, why did I choose to start drinking again? Why stop up my ears? Why bury my own words?

Humanness, I guess.

Humans walk around, being all human with each other, and we mess up—a lot. I wish I had a statistic for this, but in my own experience, I screw up about 67.2 percent of the time. Give a baby a plastic hammer and eventually, or really soon, he's going to start whacking away at everything he can find. And for a baby, it's no fun to whack away at a pillow, but when he tries it out on the cat, there's a fluffy reaction. It's more fun, but it's messing up. Just ask the cat.

We human all over each other. We crash up against and rub raw and jostle and break and make a big mess. And our messes mess with other humans, and all their messes, and so on, until infinity. Let's face it: humanity is one big bouncy house. There will be crying, or puke.

I know this is not earth-shattering, that humans screw things up a lot, but it was earth-shattering to *me*. Perhaps someone who is writing a book on humanness should not admit to missing out on this basic characteristic of humanity. What can I tell you? Brené Brown I am not.

One of my dad's favorite movies of all time is a classic western spoof called *The Hallelujah Trail*. I want to make this very clear: I am *not* recommending this movie. It's really hilarious, yes, but on the whole "let's be politically correct and not stereotype anyone" thing, it veers. However, it was made in the sixties. I mean, the father in *The Parent Trap* smoked and drank martinis throughout the entire plot, and that was with an adorable Hayley Mills around. That's a lot of veering. Anyway, *The Hallelujah Trail* stars a young and tan Burt Lancaster, and I don't care if a movie has him only standing on a chair; I would still watch it. He's dreamy.

One of the most epic scenes—from here on I will admit that I do rather love this movie; we quote it all the time in our family, which explains so much—is when a wagon train, headed by Burt and his soldiers, ends up in a sandstorm and gets attacked by the Indians, who are Native Americans in Burt-speak; sorry. The sand befuddles everyone, and they circle the wagons, randomly shoot guns and arrows, whoop and holler, drink whiskey, and ride horses right by each other in endless circles. And all the while, the unflappable narrator, who sounds a lot like Spencer Tracy, lets us know how ridiculous this is.

You had to be there, I know. It doesn't really sound all that funny, does it? Come over to our living room sometime, and we'll watch it together. You'll see. I'll even make popcorn.

The good guys and bad guys are all really within about twenty feet of each other and firing in all the wrong directions. As is so often the case in any sort of skirmish, nobody really has any idea what in the hell is going on. It's hilarious. We know that they don't know.

This is how God feels, I think. I wonder if occasionally he thinks, "Well, let me just pop some corn and have a sit-down to watch this for a bit," while we run amok.

Humanness means we wander around and lob off attacks, which are misguided and stupid, and we look so silly from above.

And humanness means we start drinking again after years of sobriety and not for any sort of reason. No one *died*. No one's cat even died. We just decided one day, "Hey, I'll drink right here! This here will be the day when I take all the work and lessons and tip them out on the floor with a crash, and other people will watch me in shock and awe. Voilà! Look at me being human all over the place!"

Now, I realize "being human" can also mean goodness, much like those posts on Facebook about people saving baby ducks from a storm drain. That's the thing about us humans. We like to do both of these things. We're baby duck people, and then we're firing at anything that moves. We like to mix it up.

You do realize that every time I spoke of "we" in this chapter, I really was sort of hoping you could come along with me on this ride. Perhaps you're saying, "Uh, no, Dana. I'm all baby duck, all the time." If that is the case, the baby ducks and I salute you.

Alas, for me, I am not a baby duck kind of person often. I apologize, sweet waterfowl. In my case, I would misfire and end up accidentally scaring the baby ducks back *into* the storm drain. Such is my luck.

It's so much more than baby ducks, though. I stubbornly insist, even with my terrible percentage of messing up, that humans—of whom I am one—have some of the greatest qualities of creatures on this Earth. We are right up there with the dolphins and those elephants that watch over orphaned baby elephants, and that cat that took in a litter of possums. Basically, we're slightly under all those animals that show kindness to other animals. So, we're about forty-seventh down on the list. But you get the idea.

We love and we mess up; we keep messing up and we keep loving. It's funny in the movies and not so funny in real life, but I'm still here and I'm still laughing. So there's that.

Now, I am off to find some baby ducks in need of help.

Conversations with God
Part One

Me: Are you there, God? It's me, Dana.

God: Let me guess, you've always wanted to say that.

Me: I loved Judy Blume as a kid.

God: Me too. Still do. Of course. That's my thing.

Me: Right. I need you to answer a question.

God: I know.

Me: Stop getting ahead of me! This is important. Can you please tell me, why does life have to be so hard? I mean, what is the point, really? Why are we here? What does it all mean? And why, please, why do I have to keep messing it all up? Why can't I get it right?

God: Whoa. That's way more than one question.

Me: Wait, there's more. Why do kids have to go hungry and why do we have to worry about bad people snatching away our children and what is going to happen to our country? We're all so mad at each other. But for now, let's just start with me.

God: Okay. Well, the straight-shot answer is love God and love others.

Me: And, let me guess, live by the Boy Scout law?

God: Well . . . if you're into camping, I guess. But really, it's all about love.

Me: That's such a Michael Bolton answer.

God: I love Michael Bolton.

Me: Of course you do. That's your thing. Listen, I'm no Mother Teresa—

(God rolls his eyes.)

Me: What I *mean* is, I can't just love others and that's it. It's too hard. And boring. Mother Teresa can do that but not me.

God: It's true. You really are no Mother Teresa. She and I had lunch today, and you certainly are not her. You're Dana. And you may find this whole loving me and loving others thing is not boring at all.

Me: Okay. But it is hard.

God: That's true. But you know what Michael Bolton said.

Me: Oh, no.

God: *(singing)* "That's what love is all about."*

Me: You didn't.

God: Yep. I sure did.

---

*Michael Bolton's album THE HUNGER *released in 1987.*

CHAPTER TEN

HOW TO
be cool

When I was a kid, I would watch my brother get ready to go out dancing on a Saturday night. He would coat himself in Brut and polyester while the Bee Gees chirped in the background. "Be cool, kid," he would say to me and then head out into the evening, trailing sophistication, and a whole lot of cheap cologne, in his wake.

I have a cinematic memory of my brother. It's illuminated with the soft-filtered light of Polaroid images where I am little and he is big. I am looking up. I have feathered hair and a lime-green terry cloth jumper, and he's getting into his souped-up Volkswagen before prom night, dressed in a white tux. He *was* John Travolta. Now, my memories of him are carefully folded and put away, but whenever I get them out they are a bit more frayed, a bit more creased around the edges. Some have fallen behind a drawer or under the dresser, lost forever.

He is stuck in my head accompanied by the *Saturday Night Fever* soundtrack, shiny polyester, and imitations of Steve Martin. Chris was a wild and crazy guy. In my memories, he is his own walking and talking greatest hits album.

Looking back now, I realize I had missed a few things. Heck, I was seven. As a seven-year-old, my understanding of my brother was a bit skewed. I realize now that Chris, even as a teenager, felt the weight of being the life of the party. There were those fights with my father. And he got a few DUIs. He dropped out of college after one year, probably due to too much partying. But as he grew older, these behaviors seemed to abate, and we all breathed a sigh of relief and filed them under "He's always funny, which means he's totally fine."

He wasn't fine. In the last ten or so years of his life, Chris started to slowly fall apart. His addiction to alcohol, which I think started for him much earlier than any of us in the family really knew, became more pronounced, more visible to those who loved him. He would gather sober time, and then he would relapse. Over and over. But, as usual, I always just figured he would get his life together.

But then, he didn't. He died.

I could rack up expensive hours with noncreepy therapists about why my brother's death still messes with me. I'm sure there are many reasons, including my fear of abandonment and my longing to control things. But ultimately, I think it's because I am addicted to stuff, too.

Alcohol, yes, but there are other things.

Like feelings.

Feelings make a great addiction. First of all, they are around all the time. Alcohol eventually runs out. But feelings? There's an endless supply. And feelings can be really endearing. So that's confusing. They love to be felt. They don't ever say, "Oh dear, I think I'm not making your headspace healthy right now. So, I'll just go over here, sit quietly, and leave you alone." Feelings like to be the life of the party.

Feelings are like that one kid whom the family takes out to the fancy restaurant. He's adorable but easily frustrated by the lack of chocolate milk on the menu. You can't acknowledge only the cuteness and filter out that he's dropping 90 percent of his meal on the floor.

Alcohol can be poured down the drain. Cigarettes can be thrown in the trash. You can cut up credit cards or turn off Wi-Fi, and, for a moment, the addiction is denied access. However, feelings are still there, sitting in a high chair, pounding on the table.

I remember going to eat with a friend of mine recently, and we sat next to a table that had a mom and five children. My friend Cara spied her first and nudged me. Cara did that eyebrow thing that made me start gaping around like Beyoncé had just walked in the door. Instead, it was only an extremely tired lady and her million children, but it was still rather awe-inspiring.

We both watched as all the children squirmed and asked their mom about fifteen thousand questions (five kids at about three thousand questions each; it's a math thing). Cara and I both felt our uteruses shrink in horror as we watched. One kid was all *Game of Thrones* at one point, sitting in his high chair and demanding applesauce so loudly that some patrons in the bar offered to get him some: "SAUCE, MOMMA. BRING FORTH DA SAUCE." I waited for someone to be sent to the dungeon, if there was a dungeon. I'm pretty sure Applebee's does that, but not this place.

And during all of this, the mom was so totally cool.

She helped with the applesauce issue. She wiped mouths. She kept one kid completely contained even though he was kind of all *Mission: Impossible,* all the time. She quelled crying and played tic-tac-toe. Somehow with no spouse, friend, nanny, or anyone nice from the general population, this momma managed her kids and actually smiled a couple of times.

And she didn't order alcohol.

When I first had kids and one made the tiniest of squeaks in a public place, I was the kind of mom who would pack him up along with the diaper bag, the toys, the blankies, the loveys, and any other "ies" that go with babies and hustle him the heck out of there, as if the baby was emitting some sort of deadly spore. I couldn't stand to be annoying. I couldn't stand for my children to be annoying. It would make me feel scared and sad, and everybody knows that scared *plus* sad is just the worst feeling.

On the other end of the continuum, that mom was able to have children in a public place and not feel scared or sad. Instead, I think, she seemed kind of . . . happy. And she ate stuff, so she was also full.

It was a glory to watch.

I pay so much attention to my feelings. And sooner or later, my feelings and I end up outside a restaurant, pacing up and down, and getting really hungry. This is not good.

ᕯ

When I relapsed, I put a choke hold on my feelings. Then, when I stopped, my feelings were unstoppered all over the place. This is normal for a person in recovery. Feelings get pushed down, and then they rush out, pell mell, and change you into a batshit crazy sober person for a while. But what was totally freaking me out was the unsettling realization that I had been pushing down on my feelings long before the relapse. I had thought I was being Super Sobriety Girl, but no. Basically, I was feeling all sorts of emotions about my failure to *feel* emotions. If you think about it too much, it will give you a headache.

It's a basic law of physics: smushed things must eventually unsmush. Once I was sober again, my feelings would spring forth and guiltily misbehave because they had been cramped and cranky. I felt bad for them, and thus they got a lot of attention.

My goodness. I had been screwing up my sober walk long before December with all this feelings stuff. It was enough to make me feel even *more* feelings, which kind of made me dizzy.

Once upon a time, I had figured that my life story would go like this: I would be a kid and then grow up, and all the time I would be a fairly good and happy person. And then, as I got older, I would continue being a good person, all the while becoming more good and happy until I died. Instead, it seemed I had been playing Chutes and Ladders with my life, scooting forward and then hurtling backward, with my feelings rolling the dice.

No wonder I always hated to play that game with my kids.

I am at the mercy of my emotions. I swing from steam cleaning my entire house to lying on the couch covered in Swiss Cake Roll crumbs. All this to and fro makes me dizzy, and I long to be cool and take in the world, just like my brother would tell me to do. Instead, I live in the world through a looking glass. All my thoughts and events reflect off the feelings I have. I slice apples for my sons' lunch, and all the while I see myself doing it, filtered through the weird light of my feelings. "I am bored," I think as I slice those awful apple slices. "Being a mom and slicing apples for lunch while your boys bicker about who got more milk is boring. I am feeling so very bored. And that makes me sad. So now I am bored and sad. This world is empty, and I am a worthless apple-slicing mom."

Who knew an apple could cause so many emotions?

I wonder if my brother had similar issues with his feelings. One of the final memories I have of him is a conversation we had at Thanksgiving dinner. I guess the word *conversation* is not quite correct. It felt, instead, like a poorly delivered monologue. I wanted to talk to him about my recovery because Chris was recently coming back from a relapse. I pictured it as a Lifetime Television moment with a sweet soundtrack that swelled at the end as we both teared up and went in for a long hug. "You're the best, Sis," Chris would have said. "I will never drink again because of what you just now said to me. Ever."

And I would have smiled and said, "Me neither. I promise. Look at how awesome we both are." Then, we would go inside and happily transfer our addictions and eat ourselves into oblivion on Mom's turkey and stuffing.

The following year he disappeared, and then he died from liver failure. If I could guess, I bet Chris paid a lot of attention to his feelings. And then, at the end, maybe he couldn't bear his feelings at all. Chris and I were so good at so many things, but feelings were not our forte.

During the actual Thanksgiving conversation, I talked about getting sober as Chris looked out to the yard, nodding once in a while. I remember Chris was suffering from a bad skin issue at the time, and he was, quite literally, not comfortable in his own skin. He would shrug his shoulders, twitch, and pull at the collar of his shirt. He didn't seem to be listening at all. That whole meaningful moment with my brother, where we bonded over addiction and the work of it and recovery, wasn't really what I had imagined. That was not the moment I was looking for.

After my relapse, I was the one looking out into the distance, shrugging and tugging at my life.

My life wasn't what I was looking for. I had really messed up and failed, and the cracks were everywhere.

As I came to find out, that was a good thing.

Conversations with God:
Part Two

Me: (*standing at the abyss*) Why? WHY DOES IT ALL HAVE TO BE SO HARD?

God: Dana, listen to me very carefully, okay?

Me: (*sniffling*) It's cold up here.

God: I love you.

Me: That's it?

God: What? You wanted some fireworks?

Me: Moses got a burning bush.

God: Dana . . .

Me: WHAT!?

God: I love you.

Me: That's great, but it doesn't answer my question.

God: I love you.

Me: And you could at least shazam me with a sweater or a pullover or something.

God: I love you.

Me: Nothing is right with me anymore.

God: I love you.

Me: Oh, all right. Enough. I love you, too. I do.
I really do.

God: I know. Loving me gives you permission to love
yourself.

Me: Oh. Wow.

God: No matter what.

Me: I NEED A TISSUE.

God: I love you.

Me: Okay. Wait. Will *that* make me feel all better? Will I
be okay? Will I? When? How? Will it be warmer then?

God: Okay, let's start again. I love you.

more

"Mom? This right here? I need it."

—MY SIX-YEAR-OLD SON,
POINTING TO A 400-DOLLAR DEATH STAR LEGO SET

CHAPTER ELEVEN

HOW TO
shop at Costco
AND NOT
give in to despair

I stared at a bag of quinoa that contained enough of the stuff to feed my family for over three years. I knew that I didn't like quinoa, but I felt like I should.

Charlie and Henry love Costco. They love the extra-largeness of it. They love the samples. They love that I can push them both in a cart, even though they have outgrown this, because Costco's carts are the size of a Smart car. I push them along with the slow-moving determination of a barge. Two children are packed inside with some quinoa and a twelve-pack of Whisker Lickins.

Costco is a place to contemplate one's life choices. It's the Grand Canyon of stuff. We have to stop and take in the scenery, maybe take a few pictures. Stuff is everywhere stacked high. Even if it's a mountain of Pedigree, it still gives one pause. Everything here is so very, very big. Addiction notices me pausing at a backyard play set that is bigger than our living room, which would mean we obviously have to purchase it and then move. Addiction says, "You should get that. You know why? It's so big. And you, my girl, are so very, very small. You need a big life because what's inside of you has become small and shriveled. Let's talk. Come over here and sit beside me for a while. Just for a while, I promise."

I give addiction a big, fat side-eye and just keep my cart moving. If I'm really feeling saucy, I call out addiction and say, "Back off. And that's total crap. I am totally fine over here. I'm having some La Croix, see? I bought a pallet of the pamplemousse flavor, which is a fruit. I think. And I'm adding a twist of lime, from this four-pound bag, okay? I'm so totally FINE. OKAY?"

A lot of limes have met a terrible end after all this fine behavior at the Costco.

It's important to note that this dialogue occurs in my head. I don't actually engage in conversation with addiction at Costco. That is reserved for when I'm at home and only have the dog as my audience. He does not judge.

I was back in therapy; Brian insisted on it. When Brian and I talked about the relapse, I could almost see the invisible clipboard in his hand as he ticked off the list of things I needed to do to get better. We were still circling each other: he with his clipboard and me with all my feelings about that clipboard.

We hadn't fought once since the blowup; however, our conversations were careful. We spoke in muted tones as though we became the background noise of the television. I wiped down the counters and folded some T-shirts while we scheduled an oil change on my car. He checked his phone and started a game of chess with Charlie. We never just sat, made eye contact, and talked. There was always something else going on.

Sadly, there was not much else going on with Brian and me. My therapist and I talked about all the relationship things I had talked about in previous sessions. I felt like my own greatest hits compilation, rehashing all our old numbers. My therapist was kind but didn't seem to like Brian much, which was weird because everyone likes Brian, including me. She kept suggesting that I was right and he was wrong. This was totally awesome, but I wondered if my words were so gunked up with feelings that right or wrong didn't really apply here. I felt like the truth was out there somewhere, wandering about, and who was right about it didn't matter. Just finding the truth, and taking it home to be safe with us, did.

I was so not loving therapy. It seemed too easy. I talked about how I was dissatisfied with my life, and my therapist agreed with me. Also, she would say things such as "And how does that make you feel, Dana?" This was confusing because she had just told me, about two minutes earlier, that Brian was wrong and I was right, so evidently that was how I should have felt. She was the expert here, and she seemed to have a solid take on the situation, so why ask me?

It takes work to organize and distribute the feelings in my brain, and so therapy feels like how I often feel about the state of my house: so overwhelmed by the mess that the only solution is to lie on the couch and watch *Say Yes to the Dress* for so long that when I finally stand up to go to the bathroom I get dizzy. I continued with my sessions because Brian asked that I do so, and I needed to do this for him. This is so totally not the reason to do therapy. When you agree to crack open your head and spill the contents, the motive should be assisting your brain, not someone else's.

Also, I needed proof. It's like teeth-whitening strips without the selfie. If you don't take a picture before you start applying the sticky Saran Wrap things to your teeth, then you just keep checking your face in your rearview mirror and peering at them with snarly focus, wondering if there is any change. I wanted a before and after shot with each therapy lesson. Instead, I got in my car, drove home, hummed along with the radio, and planned dinner. At no point did I notice anything gleaming in the mirror.

I still wanted gleaming. I wanted the big life, after all.

Big lives involve a lot of shiny.

☙

So, back at Costco, I bought my weight in quinoa. Quinoa is not shiny. It's kind of dusty, actually, but it will have to do. Charlie sat at the head of the cart like the lookout at the prow of the ship. He pointed out various treats individually packaged in crinkly wrappers. It seems— with kids anyhow—that if food is in a small, crinkly wrapper, it's tastier.

Charlie and Henry both spotted a carton of teensy Oreos packaged in teensy bags, all in a box the size of a baby elephant. Their level of distress was high because I was not buying the cutesy Oreos.

"But Mom! Lookit! THEY'RE SNACK-SIZED. They're in the little bags, see? We can take 'em places!"

Their statement was true. The tiny, crinkly bags beckoned to us, longing to be unwrapped from their aggressive overpackaging and put in a back pocket. They were so cute.

I sighed and picked up the baby elephant and put it in the cart.

The shoppers and I at Costco were choreographed in a sort of unrehearsed dance. We walked slowly, mainly due to the fact that we needed to hunch over the cart handles to keep the cart aligned so we didn't run over displays of pool floaties or the small children near them. We kept our carts at a steady pace and pivoted around each corner, glancing at each other and lifting one side of our mouths in a "Well, here we are" kind of half-assed smile. We do-si-do'd around the frozen lasagnas and dispersed again to our separate aisles with water softener or lifetime supplies of Zyrtec. And then we all gathered again at checkout, the universal weigh station for the tired and heavily burdened.

We really do like our stuff, don't we?

And we like it in bulk.

What a weird word . . . *bulk*. It means in excess or overly full. It's how a twenty-year-old kid's luggage looks like when he's coming home from college, filled to the seams with dirty Led Zeppelin T-shirts and jeans that haven't been washed for an entire semester. It's doubly distressing because those T-shirts were purchased at Target by a man-boy who wouldn't know "Whole Lotta Love" if it came up and smacked him in the ass.

Also, when I hear *bulk* I think of constipation and bulk-forming laxatives, which is so not pleasant at all. Either way, it's not optimal.

And yet, we keep buying bulk. And we cart it home, lugging it into our houses and shoving it into closets and pantries. Then, we buy more storage containers in which to put the bulk. We have bulked our bulk.

We live in a culture of more. I combat my perfectionism with more-ness. More gadgets. More cute shoes. More toys for my children. More Zoloft.

As I pushed the cart down the cereal aisle, contemplating enough Cheerios to feed a day care, I stopped. I just stopped, right in the middle of the aisle, in the way of all the other cumbersome carts, and I rested my chin on my hands.

Henry pulled his eyes away from an enticing tower of Fruit Roll-Ups and looked at me. He said in his cute Henry way, "What doin', Momma?"

I straightened up and eyed him, and then I went all Scarlet O'Hara on my children.

"As God is my witness," I said with a tremble, clutching my Costco membership card in my hand and raising it to the ceiling, "as God is my witness, I WILL NEVER SHOP AT COSTCO AGAIN!"

Okay, that's not exactly what I did, but you get the idea.

I realized that my stance against bulk was pretty illogical. My therapist, I was sure, would ask me how I felt about it. Brian, I knew, would wonder why I was avoiding the savings in toilet paper alone. But as I ferried my cart and my children out to the car, while straining against it so I didn't scrape the door of someone's bulk SUV, I had had enough. It was like I had a redeemed Grinch moment, realizing that maybe, just maybe, whatever it was I was looking for didn't come from a store, in bulk.

Every so often I get to have an ice cream dream. This is a total opposite experience to the mom-under-the-refrigerator nightmare. It is heaven. It's me and an ice cream store. As I lean over the display, staring at all the glistening chocolates and gooey strawberries, the guy behind the counter says, "You can have anything you like. Today, it's free." The really amazing part of the dream is my reaction to this. I don't freak out or start shoveling all the flavors into one wheelbarrow-sized bowl. Instead, I carefully walk back and forth, perusing all the colors and smells. Often my children are with me, and we ask for samples and analyze our favorites like little dairy epicureans.

I have noticed that I get to have this dream about once a month, right in concert with other hormonal cycles I have the pleasure of entertaining. My uterus is thoughtful, I guess. At any rate, once the ice cream is selected—I'm feeling like some mocha fudge—I sit down at one of those spindly little tables they always have at these shops. And I get out my spoon and dip it in the bowl and then . . . nothing. I wake up. Or that dream ends, and the next one is queued up, usually the one about me doing laundry or buttering toast.

I never get to actually eat the mocha fudge.

Here's the thing. I don't even mind. It's the selecting that is so fun, the walking back and forth past the tubs of vanilla walnut and pink bubble gum. It's fun to window-shop. Granted, it's a dream, so eating the stuff might actually end up weird. Dreams do that. My mocha fudge might end up tasting like cotton balls, or my mom's oyster dressing, or some other concoction tied to my psyche. I'll never know. And still, I look forward to the dream. It's the most fun I've had in a long time.

And so, I vowed to live like that. Like I'm in that ice cream shop, looking at all the colors and breathing in the sugared air. If you've ever watched a three-year-old eat a scoop of birthday cake ice cream, you know. That's how we should do it. We shouldn't stop to ask ourselves how we're feeling about the sprinkles. We should just eat it and make a mess, and when we're full, wipe off and take a nap. I think my dream keeps trying to remind me of that.

So, I vowed to eat more ice cream and stop shopping in bulk. It's the weirdest combination of self-help out there. I don't think anyone has ever suggested it in any behavior modification or talk-therapy setting before, but I don't care. Because, you know what?

It started working.

It really started working.

Items Best
Bought in Bulk

1. Thank-you cards.

2. Gift wrap—not those silly bags but shiny wrapping paper. The kind you rip.

3. Ribbons.

4. Kazoos and Silly String.

5. Party hats and tiaras. Especially tiaras.

6. Balloons, helium optimal.

7. Cupcake sprinkles.

8. Hugs.

9. Kisses.

10. Life.

CHAPTER TWELVE

HOW TO BE
married and content
AT THE
same time

Based on the title of this chapter, it would be safe to assume that I am going to jump right in and talk about my very important bond with my beloved husband. You would be wrong. For the first few pages I would really much rather tell you all about my relationship with my cat, Bob.

Bob is a tiny, grey cat who lives in our house, I swear. I say this because my friends have never actually seen Bob. She hides. Yes, Bob is a she. She earned her name because she is missing almost all of her tail. Also, she has feline influenza, so I have to give her daily meds, and sometimes I can be caught saying things such as "Can you grab me a tissue? I've got to go wipe Bob's nose." Perhaps due to all of this, Bob is extremely shy around humans and rarely can anyone in our household spy her, unless she is skulking past in her weird, skittery way as if she is saying, "DON'T LOOK AT ME. LOOK AWAY, LOOK AWAY."

This cat, in sum, is kind of a mess.

And I loooooove her.

Every night, as I tuck myself into bed, I feel a soft pounce on the bed. Bob is ready for bed too. She will slowly walk up my side until she has managed to wedge her tiny, nervous greyness as firmly into my side as possible, and there she will remain until morning. Or until I roll over on her, which has happened. She didn't really do much; she just flattened herself out like roadkill, waiting until I realized that I was crushing the life out of her. She has really sharp little hip bones, so I did finally wake up, and she slid out of the bed. I swear I heard her murmur, "No, really, that's all right. I'm fine. I just need to go walk it off. I'll be right back. Cheery-bye." And yes, in my mind, Bob speaks like she's Angela Lansbury; it suits her somehow. Perhaps it's because once I tried to dress her up in a doily and a tea cozy, but she doesn't like to talk about that.

Bob doesn't talk at all, which is another reason why I love her so. She doesn't even meow. The most noise we ever hear out of her is a sneeze, delicate and phlegmy.

On occasion I like to call her Silent Bob, but it doesn't really make her all that happy. She's not a Gen X cat. That's Steve, our white behemoth who lies around all day, makes a lot of noise, and is mellow about everything. He has no personal aspirations and is such a happy cat that Bob walks by him and eyes him with total suspicion. I have actually seen him put his paw around her shoulders and lick her ear as if to say, "Relax, lady. Chilly-chill. It's all good. Here, lemme get you a tissue."

The truth is, Bob has issues. She has a dark past. This makes me love her all the more, of course. She is not at all like Hosmer, our dog, or pretty much anyone else in this house. Hosmer hangs out, waits for his next meal, and is so jazzed when the meal comes that he can't even eat it, he's just so grateful. He loves it when people just walk past him. "Hey!" he says with a wag as they pass by, "You are so awesome for doing that! For the walking! See you again soon!" Hosmer's life goals are to lean on me and, if I move, quickly lick the moving part of me. His deepest secret is where he has hidden his squeaky carrot toy. And it's right on his bed, in full view.

I don't really know what Bob has hidden in her past. I received her from a friend who wasn't able to care for her anymore. It seems Bob has been fostered quite a bit. We don't know how she lost her tail, but I don't think these things happen pleasantly.

I just know. I look into her deep, slightly cross-eyed face with her little tongue sticking out just a little, and I just know. She has a dark past. She's *seen things*. And then, I get up to get a tissue because I need to wipe her nose.

I know some would say that my relationship with my wheezy cat is a bit strange, but ours is a love without borders. Or normality, it seems. But she just needs me so much. When the boys go to bed, Bob shows up, walking up to me with her crossed eyes and her bowlegged strut. She sits so close I can feel her take a breath, in and out. I am the only one she will sit, or sneeze, upon.

It's nice to be so needed. I just wish it wasn't so phlegmy.

True, my kids need me. But that's in an "I'm your kid and need you, but I will also drive you bonkers due to my ability to talk about Jar Jar Binks for hours with barely a break for air" kind of way. Bob is so very quiet. She asks for a bowl of kibble and the occasional tissue. And I'm pretty sure she agrees with me on the whole Jar Jar thing, so we're good.

Brian doesn't need me. I know; that sounds kind of harsh. But I have come to realize that marriages are not based on the super romantic, "You are my sun, my moon, my everything" kind of thing. I mean, Brian does love me. And he does, I guess, need me. But he doesn't *need* me. Not like Bob does, anyway.

⌒

Are you familiar with that scene from *Jerry Maguire* where Tom makes cinema gold and tells what's-her-face that she completes him? That scene has messed up so many marriages. This is why it makes it so easy to dislike Tom Cruise for a lot of things.

Brian and I watched *Jerry Maguire* together. It was a romantic night, with popcorn, sex on the first date (theirs), and bed at 10:00 p.m. sharp (ours).

As we prepared for bed, Brian and I embarked on a long discussion about why I should stop buying bargain toilet paper. I don't know how we got there. Something about "You had me at hello" got us into a conversation that had subpoints and follow-up arguments on two-ply. I think, at one point, Anderson Cooper was called in to moderate.

"What you are failing to acknowledge," Brian said, his hands folded in a tent with fingers aligned, "is that my derriere* can only tolerate super soft. Not sandpaper."

"Yes, I get that, because I know how important your derriere is to you. Like, really important. But, honey, I am not going to buy it in bulk. We talked about this."

"Yeah, your whole refusal-to-go-to-Costco thing. What was that about again? I don't get why you would do that. Our children need gigantic bags of cereal to feed them. Don't you want to feed them?"

"Your love of Costco toilet paper is what is driving the argument here, not our children and not finances. Just that stupid toilet paper. And yes, I won't go back to Costco. I hate it there."

"Right. You had some sort of epiphany at Costco. And so, I have

---

*   *Not the word actually used. Trying to class it up a bit.*

sandpaper for my derriere, and it's killing me. I am going to die a slow, sandpapered death."

"Is it a tiny bit possible that you are overexaggerating here?"

"No, I'm not."

"Yes, you are. And it's exfoliating."

"NOBODY NEEDS EXFOLIATION DOWN THERE."

⌒

All the while, during this scintillating debate, Hosmer sat at our feet and quivered with distress. He sensed the growing frustration over paper products in our house, and his anxiety levels were sparking around in his tiny brain. Bob, on the other hand, folded herself into my side and sneezed occasionally with bliss. She didn't pay much attention to the argument, except when I shifted in my seat and she had to come along for the ride. She's like those remora fish that attach to the side of whales . . . but furry.

I bet Jerry Maguire never argued about toilet paper.

Well, maybe. He does seem rather intense. Perhaps these things matter to him.

Our marriage seems to have tides. Every marriage does. We ebb and we flow with our feelings for each other and hope we don't wreck. And our marriage has steered past many dangerous waters: my growing addiction; his anger issues—oh, and I'm sure those first two are so not linked—my relapse; and his innate desire to eat gas station hot dogs even though I beg him not to. And here we are, still floating along. We might be clutching onto stray driftwood, but we are still alive. And we are still in love, or working at being in love, every day.

Brian was not quite as enthusiastic about my recovery the second time around. I wasn't either. On more than one occasion, I missed a meeting because he got home late.

"Where R U?" I texted. There was no response until he showed up as I paced the floor in the kitchen.

"I had a meeting tonight, remember?"

He looked at me blankly for a minute then rubbed his hand through his hair. "I am so sorry. I forgot. Can you still go?"

"No. It's okay. I'll make sure to put it on the calendar next time."

And so it went. However, before Brian came home I was frustrated and wanted to add to the conversation, making addenda to the text that I actually sent.

"WHY CAN'T . . ."

"IT'S ALWAYS WEDNESDAY, HOW HARD . . ."

"IT'S NOT ROCKET SCIENCE, FOR THE LOVE OF . . ."

I started each of those texts but didn't complete any of them because Brian and I were being extra kind to each other. And most of the time, texts like that only add mean to angry, and that's just dumb. If you're going to start out at angry, you don't need to add anything to it. That's like pouring Tabasco all over Brian's five-alarm chili, when honestly, the chili was already its own advertisement for Pepto-Bismol.

Also, never, ever text in all caps. Like, ever.

Instead, I made sure to remind him or to set up a sitter, and I kept going to meetings. I didn't give up in a huff and start drinking Jägermeister just so I could make a point to Brian. That is precisely how the alcoholic in me would operate, and I don't listen to her anymore—she's crazy.

Brian and I weren't having any more colossal fights, which was boring and good at the same time. Boring and good was a theme I was going for. I kept the house tidy. I started writing again. I didn't forget to pay the auto insurance, and I made appointments for the dentist. I wrote detailed lists of what my day would entail at the beginning of the week and then carefully checked off each item. Sometimes I even used colored pens. Each day was like one of those ubiquitous "keep calm" graphics.

I hugged Brian when he came home, and he kissed me goodnight, and we continued to walk along. No major icebergs floated by. The waves were still.

It was all so dull I wanted to scratch my eyes out.

But wait. Valentine's Day was coming.

As is so often the case, Valentine's Day ends up being the lame spinoff of the winter holidays. Halloween, Thanksgiving, and Christmas are the trilogy of fun. They involve costumes, men in costumes, candy, and presents. Thanksgiving doesn't really have all that, and its main color scheme is brown. But it has pies and a parade. And did I mention, pie?

Valentine's Day has love, but in my opinion that does not compete with reindeer that fly.

I did know better than to plan a Fantastically Romantic Evening (FRE). I didn't really know what an FRE was anymore since Brian and I were both harboring small children. They had pretty much beaten the romantic out of us. We looked at them, particularly after watching them fight about who has a milliliter more of chocolate pudding and four more sprinkles, and we knew the truth: romantic was what caused all of this. Romantic was evil.

But I did want to do something notable. I felt like I needed it. And Brian, too.

The thing is, I love him. And Valentine's Day is all queued up for that.

Because I always think I am way more Pinterest-y than I actually am, I signed up to bring cupcakes to Charlie's class for Valentine's Day. In my mind, that always seemed like such a great idea because I would be helping in the classroom but not during the time-sucking nuttiness of the holiday trinity. This was also fortuitous because I didn't really know I was going to relapse during the holidays, and now I was sober and making cupcakes, all at the same time. Thus, I would be able to make the cupcakes with the relaxed ease of a sober Martha Stewart. The only difference would be that I would be wielding store-bought frosting. Sorry, Martha.

I decided to make a double batch of the cupcakes and incorporate them into my Valentine's Day with Brian. Then, I planned to make Brian's favorite dinner. For the evening's festivities, we would eat steak and cupcakes and then watch a movie.

I know. I want to curl up and take a nap just writing this.

I had wanted to curl up and take a nap for so long, and Valentine's Day was no different. But this is marriage. You get up and kiss each other hello, with his stubble and your morning breath. And he makes the coffee too weak, and you forget to pick up the towels, and his lunch is leftover chili that wasn't good on the first running. And you text each other about four times each day, but it's mainly about whether you paid the water bill or whether he can pick up dog food. And a lot of times the texts are answered with "Y," which is code for "I'm too busy to talk and I don't want to text 'K' because that's rude, but somehow I can't even get the time to push 'E' and 'S.'" Your discussions at night hit maybe ten minutes tops. Instead, you invest in long-winded conversations with small children about why peeing is a sport that involves both aim and dedication. And then you fall asleep, but not before he smushes over and tries to kiss your cheek but ends up kissing your eyeball due to the light being turned off. Then he snores and you hog the blankets. And you get up and do the whole thing again the next day. And so on.

That's marriage. It's built upon a foundation of "and so on."

I realize I am not really selling this whole marriage thing. It doesn't make an inspiring bumper sticker—Marriage: Sometimes It's Nice.

I would say Brian and I have a comfortable marriage. Comfortable is not bad. Slippers are comfortable. So are large couches and smooth jazz channels on the radio. And honestly, if I must, I'll compare my marriage to warm, fuzzy slippers anytime. There are worse things. Yet, contentment doesn't have to live in fuzzy slippers. It can live in Manolos, or some other high-end footwear; however, I don't wear Manolos because they make my toes feel like they're being eaten by stylish piranhas.

Contentment deserves better.

When I first got married, I wanted big feelings. If I'd had the choice, I would have picked the overacted, standing-on-the-roof-of-Alcatraz, holding-up-flares-and-shouting-my-lines type of feelings. I wanted to be the Nicolas Cage of marriages. To this day, I still don't know what to do with feelings that are on low volume. But I'm learning to work with them.

I have a friend whose parents are so in love it's ridiculous. They finish each other's sentences and like to sit on each other. One is always stroking the other like they need to be scratched behind the ears. They are so attentive all the time, bringing each other drinks or small plates of crackers and cheese.

It's really kind of gross.

Granted, they really do seem to genuinely like each other, but the fact that they follow each other around like puppies is terrifying.

I mean, what will happen when one of them up and *dies*? What then, cheese-and-cracker guy?

You know what I also have a hard time with? Those Hallmark cards that have pink roses all over them and the swoopy gold raised letters saying, "You Are My World, Please Don't Ever Leave Me." I don't like those cards. They are too much. When you open the card, you have to get that weird smile on your face and pretend to read the four paragraphs of redundancy inside while your husband watches you to see if he made you cry. It's uncomfortable. Those cards just seem too . . . needy.

What's comfortable is a marriage based not on *need* but on interdependence.

I know. I sound so super healthy and also really coldhearted here, don't I? Stay with me.

It only took me about ten years of marriage to get to this point. Brian, not so much. He was pretty cool with the fact that I was not the wind beneath his wings from the start. I don't know how he got to be all self-aware from the get-go. It's kind of annoying.

All this not-needing business leaves a great big hole to be filled by God, which is a good thing. Need doesn't have to be synonymous with love here. I *need* oxygen, but I don't *loooooove* it. I don't take selfies with it or write about it in my journal or plan trips to go visit oxygen. Yet I desperately need it.

On the other hand, I really like Brian.

It's a good thing, too, because if I needed him he would totally piss me off, like *all* the time. He says things to me when he comes to bed really late and I'm fast asleep such as "Have the cats been down in the crawl space? It smells like it." Then, I'm on cat patrol in my head at one o'clock in the morning. But I don't desperately need him, so when he does this I can smush at his face with my hand and say things such as "Don't speak. Talk tomorrow. Sleep now." Brevity is my thing after 10:00 p.m.

I don't need him, but I like that he's around. On a cold night, he allows me to tuck my feet between his calves when he gets in bed, even at 1:00 a.m. He doesn't even twitch. He just kind of sighs with resignation and deals with the frostbite. And I just really like hanging with Brian. He makes me laugh. He likes to sing along in the car to classic rock and has a rather nutty conviction that he has the vocal cords of Roger Daltry. It makes for a good show. Talent or not, he has a lot of gusto, and this, I think, is the essence of our union.

Yep. That's what it is: the goofy factor. It's what makes our marriage tick. Think about it. If you had a union with someone who was constantly deep and constantly soul-searching, and had emotive goo slathered all over it, wouldn't you go kind of nutty after a while?

In sum, this is not my marriage. We don't do goo. We go through endless arcs. We think each other kind of adorable. Then, we can't stand each other. This is followed by wallowing in apathy. And then, we cycle back again. Marriage to my husband is generally good, generally positive, and often, very specifically maddening. Perfect wives don't exist, and neither do perfect husbands, but we stay together. This is a straight-up miracle. Most marriages are.

But then, watching my husband play air guitar to "Shine on You Crazy Diamond" reminds me that youth is fleeting.

But nuttiness?

It's forever.

If My Marriage Was
a Nicolas Cage Movie

Me: Did you remember to bring home dog food?

Brian: Dana! I love you! I love you! Always! *(chopper sounds in the background)* I'm sorry I was late. I was saving people.

Me: Good job, honey. But the dog food?

Brian: ALWAYS AND FOREVER I WILL LOVE YOU.

Me: Okay, but I just need a roger on the dog food? The dog is eyeing the kids.

Brian: Never! I'll protect them. Of course. And hold on! Just wait there! Wait for me!

Me: For the . . . food? Or you? Are you going?

Brian: Wait for me!

Me: A large portion of my life seems to be waiting for you, dear.

Brian: I love you! I need you!

Me: And an Uzi doesn't work with conceal and carry, Brian. Give it.

Brian: I'm going out there! For the dog food! But I will come back! This is really important! Our lives are in the balance!

Me: JUST THE DOG'S, REALLY.

(*Brian does a tuck and roll to the back door and peers out.*)

Me: See? If you had tried that with your Uzi, I know you would have hurt yourself. It's bulky.

Brian: Maybe I should wait until dark. I spot a bogey at twelve o'clock.

Me: That's the dog. He's the one holding up a sign that says, "Will work for food." My goodness, this thing is heavy. Nobody likes an Uzi, honey. Just stop.

Brian: Hold on! Let me just light this flare . . .

Me: NOT IN THE HOUSE. HOW MANY TIMES DO I HAVE TO TELL YOU? JUST GO OUTSIDE. NOW. OUTSIDE NOW.

Brian: Okay, but stay here! I'm going out there! (*a lot of gesturing*) You stay right here!

(*Brian comes in for a kiss. The music swells and chopper wind tosses my hair like I'm Penélope Cruz. I'm really tan. Brian's mullet flutters in the breeze.*)

Me: Wow! I love you! I'll wait! Forever, darling! Be careful! Go, GO!

CHAPTER THIRTEEN

HOW TO

escape

YOUR

family

I was in a taxi headed to my speaking gig in Florida. Palm trees pulsed past my window. Everything looked like a postcard, with flowers dripping from trees and a sky the color of a swimming pool. My driver was a man named Jim. He told me that I was his last fare because his daughter was getting married today.

"This is good luck! What a great way to start my trip. Congratulations!" I tell him.

Jim kind of grunted. I waited for him to follow up on this but no luck. So, I looked out the window, trying to spy some flamingos. There were always flamingos in *Miami Vice,* which is my only understanding of Florida. I started to ask Jim where all the flamingos were, but he spoke first. I think he figured it was time to start in on the polite banter.

"So, what brings you to Florida?"

I took a breath and started my spiel. "I'm an author. And speaker. About recovery. So, I'm here to speak. About recovery."

I have learned to make sure to tack on the subject of my speaking at the beginning, or there is awkwardness. Or more awkwardness. If

I simply say that I am an author, this elicits much enthusiasm. I think people go immediately to the idea that I am J. K. Rowling. And then, when I explain that I write and speak about being an alcoholic mom in recovery, the happy visions of Hogwarts thunk to the floor. I see their shoulders slump a little. I watch them try to come up with an enthusiastic response, such as "Great job, you . . . alcoholic, you!" It just gets weird.

I decided to ask Jim about the wedding.

Jim shrugged. "It's not her first one." I didn't really even know how to respond. Was this bad? Good? Is she widowed? Did she collect marriages? What tone do I take here? Jim saved me from responding by unloading the entire story. The floodgates had opened.

"Yeah. This is her third one. The third. That's supposed to be a charm, right?"

I nodded vehemently.

"Yeah, so she's twenty-two. And seven months pregnant. Third marriage."

I just kept nodding and, like a bobblehead, kept doing so for pretty much the rest of the trip.

"Nope. Not her first. Not her first kid, either. But luckily, the first one isn't with this guy. This guy . . ." Jim waved his hand around like the groom was somehow circling the top of the Cadillac, and he wanted to swat at him. "He's kind of a scumbag. At least that's what I think, but what do I know? She loves him. Whatcha gonna do?"

I scrabbled around in my brain for the appropriate response. My condolences? Good luck? Is it chicken or fish on the menu?

When we stopped, he showed me a picture of the couple on his phone.

"They're getting married at the beach. It's supposed to rain. This is their engagement photo." He said "PHO-to" as he poked at the picture.

The image showed a blonde, pregnant girl who looked about twelve in the arms of a man in a white tank top and baggy shorts who looked sinewy and tired. They both had a lot of tattoos, and neither one of them was smiling. As if to embellish this, Jim stated, "They both got issues. She's a wild one. Drugs. You know."

I nodded more. Jim added, "He just got outta rehab. He just lost his job. And they're moving in with me. But anyhow, lemme get your bags. . . . Welcome to St. Petersburg!"

"Well. I bet she has a great dress," I replied as I headed inside the hotel. And I silently prayed for Jim as I rolled my suitcase to the front desk. I swear I heard a thunderclap as I did. Poor Jim.

And then, I made it to my hotel room. It was a dream. It had a balcony overlooking the pool and a huge bed with creamy-white sheets and gigantic pillows. There was thick, soft carpeting and a bathroom that echoed. It was a palace. When I walked from one room to the other, I heard nothing. The carpet absorbed all the sound. And then there was the television. Actually there were two of them, with two remotes, and each television had about 600 channels, give or take a few.

I headed to the window and opened the double doors to the balcony with a flourish, which was something I had always wanted to do, by the way. I swear I heard a Disney song in the background, and I started fluttering my hands at my eyes, muttering, "I swore I wasn't going to cry!" For a good twenty minutes it was just me, my cup of coffee, and the strangers in the pool below. I sat there, looking out at the palm trees and breathing in the soft, wet Florida air. Far off, there was a wedding occurring that didn't seem to have a chance in hell, but still. I started to hum "Can You Feel the Love Tonight." This, quite simply, was paradise.

I know this all sounds a bit melodramatic. But I was having a moment—with a hotel room.

My hotel room was all, "Heeeeyyy you. Come sit down and drink coffee with me. This will be the hot kind that you never have to reheat because Henry interrupted you mid-sip to look for a Lego that's the size of an aspirin and you left your mug in the microwave. You always find it there, all cold and alone, the next morning. It's your thing." Ah, hotel room. You knew me so well. And then hotel room said, "Also, you can watch romantic comedies. There's about seven of them on right now, all at the same time. At least two have Ryan Gosling in them. And not once will anyone change the channel to sports or anything with a Jar Jar in it."

Six hours later, I was lying amongst crumpled Blow Pop wrappers and had watched fourteen episodes of *Diners, Drive-Ins and Dives*. I couldn't seem to turn away from the host of this show. His bleached hair was hypnotic. And the last episode involved a meatball sub that was about as delicious as this hotel room.

When I rolled over to exit the bed, a sticky Blow Pop wrapper attached itself to my backside. Hotel Room and I were now in the part of the relationship where we started to pass gas and walk around with our guts hanging out. We were clearly taking advantage of each other.

I wandered into the bathroom to take a shower that lasted longer than all my showers in a week back home. I also cranked the air conditioning to the point where I could nearly see my breath. Hotel Room knew this was just a way to get back at the fact that I slept with a man who was his own thermonuclear device at night. Brian emanates so much heat that it is like sleeping with a snoring bedroll who also wants to cuddle and sweat on you.

By the next morning, Hotel Room and I were kind of on the outs. I stayed awake until nearly 1:00 a.m. because *Property Brothers* just kept going, sucking poor, hapless people in with the granite countertops and stainless steel everything before telling them they couldn't afford it. It was cruel. Every time, the people absolutely fell in love with the house, and then the brothers sat there with their puppy-dog eyes and said, "Nope. Can't have it. Like, ever. I bet you're really surprised, huh?"

I couldn't stop watching. In fact, the television played on throughout the night, something I had been taught was one of the seven deadly sins—right next to standing in front of an open fridge—and when I woke up, I felt rumpled. My teeth were fuzzy from the Blow Pop residue. I had a headache from the buzzy television and nearly freezing overnight. In other words, I had a hangover from my hotel room.

My relapse was long gone. I was writing and speaking about recovery. I was such a sober rock star. And right now, I was kind of a mess. In a sticky kind of way.

And that was all right.

It was just fine, in fact.

⌒

Balance is for gymnasts. It's not for me. Gymnasts are tiny and chirpy, and they can fly. I don't need that kind of activity level in my life. Balance tells me to take all the weight of my life—my to-do lists, the endless laundry, and all those requests from people needing me to find things—and spread them out so they're evenly distributed. This is just a bit depressing. Also, it's nearly impossible, so then balance basically sticks its fingers in its ears and waggles them at me. Balance is like that. It's so immature.

Balance is for tennis shoes that I thought used to be for old ladies walking at the mall.

Balance is for some sort of scary margarine spread that has more chemicals in it than Chernobyl. Spread it on your toast, and it glows. Balance is dangerous.

I have a friend, Tricia, who teaches yoga classes in our town. Tricia is a kindred spirit because she has a searing sense of humor. We see each other when we pick up the kids, and she works at city hall, so whenever I pay my utility bill, there she is, smiling at me. We wave and I do a little dance because I am goofy, and she laughs. She doesn't mind the dance; she knows it's my way of dealing with leaving money behind. Anyway, Tricia also happens to be beautiful and muscled and really good at balance. She can do all those sinewy, impossible yoga moves with the cool names such as Standing Without Falling Over Crane and Look, I'm Still Not Falling Over Lotus Tiger. I don't hate her for it; she can't help it that she is making my theory about balance topple over a little. Tricia wouldn't topple. She's too light on her feet for that. And balance-y.

The thing is, when I have watched even the best yogis, I look for the wobble. I look for the slight catch in their steps. The adjustments. The half steps. The stretch and pull. None of it is perfect. It can't be, or we couldn't reach for something further out, beyond us.

And yet, I am a bit jealous of Tricia and her nearly perfect headstand. I've seen her do it. It is graceful and only a little wobbly. It is beautiful. It's why I love the ballet or looking up when snow is falling. It's a deep breath. It's Chopin.

When a singer holds a note, or a swan princess leaps, it cracks us open a little. The note stops. The dancer lands. The ground always comes up to meet us. And that is how balance is impossible. Suspension is exhaustion. At some point, we must put down the weight and anticipate another time when that chord will sound. The waiting is what makes this world bearable, the knowing it might come again.

I say we trade in our perfect balancing acts for a scheduled running away. It's where we drop all the bags we packed and take leave of our senses and run outside at night, perhaps to look up at the snow falling. It makes no sense, and that is all right. We have taken leave of our senses.

Granted, my hotel room wasn't total nirvana. It was just a lovely, lonely place where I had no dirty socks on the floor, no dinners to make, and a huge bed all to myself. We moms need to get away. We all need to be alone at times, away from family and obligations and endless expectations. When that perfection alarm starts clanging at me, paired with a loud reverberation of mom guilt and exhaustion, that's when I need to head for the hills. It's good for my parenting and for my marriage. We can't always book a trip to Florida, but a half day at a coffee shop might suffice. But I still believe a hotel room for a mom once every six months or so is a great life insurance policy, not just for the mom, but for her children and husband. Pets too.

And so, I woke up with the hotel hangover. As I rolled my suitcase down to the lobby, I made sure I didn't have Blow Pop wrappers stuck to my shoes. There was no balance here. I stayed up too late and ate too much sugar. And as I walked, I found my steps quickening because I was going home. I missed my husband and boys. The unhinging from reality set me back down, gently, to macaroni and cheese, socks on the floor, arguing about ridiculous things, pushing back the hair from fevered foreheads, and prayers.

Endless prayers.

I usually pray for my boys to be kind and strong. I pray they won't get cancer or bullied or run over by college kids in trucks that barrel down our street. I pray that they will learn how to say "I'm sorry" in a way that is believable 90 percent—okay, maybe 70 percent—of the time. I pray for Brian and me to stay alive and take care of them for a little while longer, even though we are so tired. My prayers swing from holy reverence to terror in a breath. Sometimes, I mutter "God, grant me the freaking serenity . . ." at my children because they are messing with the last, tiny, frayed shred of it.

The thing is, I have to pray. Life is hard enough. Prayer is my way of saying, "I don't have to hold up all the bags. I can put them down." It's not balanced. It's not perfect. It's just real.

Also, God is mystical. If magic really exists—the whole sparkly, weird, alive, tingly kind—it's God's department. I am so on board with that. Alcohol used to make me feel the most alive and lifted up. But it's just a freak show of lights, mirrors, and tricks in comparison to the real magic that is God. He offers flight lessons, but then he sets us down. He's real. But he's also magic. This is not logical, and it makes perfect sense. All at the same time.

When I was sixteen I was in love. When I look back on that relationship, it always seems to be cloaked in warm summer nights and Spandau Ballet. We would go out in his jeep, and I would hold his hand as he shifted gears—he would lay his hand over mine as he grasped the stick shift, which seemed so romantic then. Now, I remember and roll my eyes. Sexual frustration is so cute when you're sixteen.

I really did love him, even though I was so young. My life seemed tethered to him somehow. I walked through my days at high school with my Trapper Keeper clutched to my chest and my poofy bangs, and I always knew where he was. I always knew if he could see me. I would so often position myself in a way that he could see me. He had to see me.

If he didn't, I might disappear or float away. The grip of his hand kept me safe.

You better believe, if *Jerry Maguire* had been around back then, I would have written "You complete me" in gel markers all over my notebooks. It would have been my battle cry for making it through high school. It would have been the best I could do at the time. Instead,

I had *The Princess Bride* and John Hughes and Depeche Mode crooning about wanting to share the rest of my life with somebody. My whole life seemed to be a lean in toward this boy. He *was* the rest of my life.

But he was just a boy. He had no idea he had such status. He was royalty. Poor kid.

And yes, it wasn't healthy and it wasn't balanced. But what I heard in contrast was, "Be practical, Dana. Do the right thing, Dana. Be less passionate, Dana." And those words seemed like death to me. They seemed sane, balanced, and boring.

So, one night we were out, driving through the summer warmth and listening to Echo and the Bunnymen. We were searching for a park, someplace to hold hands and walk and probably make out until our lips were swollen. We found a park and a path and headed off into the dusk.

And that's when magic happened. We turned a corner, and there it was: a field of fireflies, all in concert, hovering above the grass and below the overhang of the trees. There were so many of them, it looked like God had strewn diamonds down upon us. And I stood there. I let go of my boyfriend's hand and just looked. I said, "Just look at it." And we obeyed.

It was romantic, but it had nothing to do with my boyfriend. I forgot he was there, just for a moment; it was lovely to stand there alone, filled up by this love note from God. It's nearly thirty years later, and I remember that field and those fireflies as if it were yesterday. As we stood on that path in the still heat of a summer night, God spoke. He said, "It will take you a long time to let go of those things you cling to so tightly. Until then, remember this night. It's a calling card. One day, you are going to realize I am more magical than that boy by your side."

And that moment and those fireflies? They completed me.

There was still hope for me.

Magical Things

1. Children sleeping.

2. Casablanca.

3. The Grand Canyon.

4. Annie Lennox.

5. When my cat folds his paws under him and sits like a furry meatloaf.

6. Biblical comprehension.

7. Fire pits and s'mores.

8. Love, when it's done right.

9. Life, when it's really valued.

10. Loss, because it helps us realize how strong we really are.

CHAPTER FOURTEEN

HOW TO
fire
YOUR
inner bartender

I used to visit my inner bartender from time to time, when I could grab a moment alone. This meant, for the most part, that my bartender and I would meet up in my bathroom.

Often this meeting occurred around 4:00 p.m. Something happens to small children at four in the afternoon. Some sort of virus sets them off, and they start lurching around, out for blood. By the time the credits roll—around 8:00 p.m., at bedtime—windows have been boarded up, and there is a lot of screaming.

The pathetic truth is that about the only time I don't multitask is when I am in the bathroom. I know, it's rather graphic; but it's true. If I could figure out a way to clean the bathroom while sitting *in* the bathroom, I would attempt it. That is how moms do things. Statistics show that moms, on the average, are enmeshed in forty-seven different activities at the same time. Twelve of those involve bleach. It's possible I don't have the exact numbers on this because I've been too busy doing forty-six other things to check. But I'll get to it.

The bathroom is quiet. It has a door and a lock, and when I go in there I am completely still. I kind of have to be, or I'll have to add "reclean the bathroom" to my list of forty-seven things. I find this time alone to be wonderful and peaceful and lovely—for about five seconds. Then, I find it alarming. As I start thinking for a few minutes in the quiet, my mind becomes a roulette wheel, slowly ticking past and landing on unpleasant moments, such as burning the dinner the previous night, Brian seeming distant, and the cat puking on the carpet again.

I know. I should not sit still. Perhaps this is why men are known for being less "thinky" about things. They don't slump on the toilet and have an existential crisis all at the same time. I once tried to explain all my existential drama while sitting still to Brian, and he got that weird look on his face that happens when I try to describe why sunsets make me sad.

"Why? Why would they make you sad, Dana? They're beautiful. Beautiful is good, right?" He blinked at me and spoke slowly.

I responded, just as slowly, "I know. And that makes me sad, okay? It's just too much."

"Too much? The pinkness? And clouds? The birds?"

I nodded solemnly.

He blinked again and said, "I gotta go to the bathroom." Then he left. The man is a cretin.

My emotional relationship with my bathroom is weird, maybe. But this happens also when we "thinky" people get into bed. I seldom find myself tucked in without at least two books, my iPad, and music. If I just lie there, eyes open and staring at the ceiling, that's when I decide we need to install a rain barrel because we are wasting water and killing the planet. Yet, if we do so, we might have more mosquitos, and we'll get the West Nile virus. Which means I need to start researching repellant that won't give us cancer. So, in sum, we need to overhaul the entire backyard and put in a compost bin while we're at it because that's what good people do.

If I stop to really think about it, I realize that I am not so much a good person. I don't turn off lights when I leave the room. I keep forgetting to tithe. I feel really sorry for homeless cats, but if somebody asks me to donate to something that is not cute or furry, I hesitate. The other day my kid walked right into a wall, and I snickered.

Also, don't get me started on the state of my kitchen floor way back in the corners. Reprehensible.

Silence is a trigger. So is stillness.

And triggers are a problem.

෴

I have fired a gun only once in my life. In my twenties, I had a friend who loved to hunt. He took me out one afternoon to his father's farm, and we set up a shooting range. It was a fence with a tin can, and it was all very *Gunsmoke* but with way worse aim. When my friend brought the gun to me, I was surprised by its heft. It felt like an oily weight in my hand.

"When you lift and aim, that's when you place your finger on the trigger," he instructed. "It's very important that you don't touch it otherwise."

"Obviously," I said.

"Obviously. Now, just lift up the gun, aim, and breathe. And then, squeeze."

I did as he told me and wondered if I had the hidden talents of a gunslinger—if somehow I would become Dirty Harry with one gunshot. I lifted the gun, aimed, and breathed. And then, I squeezed.

Turns out, shooting a gun is not my thing. It scared the crap out of me. I did manage to decimate a tuft of grass. Plus, the gun made my wrist hurt. My friend looked at me expectantly as though this shooting thing was transformative.

Yoga is transformative. A good massage is transformative. A really hot cup of coffee at 7:00 a.m. can set me right again. But guns? Not so much. However, I do acknowledge that when I was squeezing that trigger, I felt the weight behind it. There is a lot of power in a single movement that is enough to kill a living thing. It's a burden. The trigger, the target, and the gun are all burdens.

A trigger can be the silence of a room—after you have spent the entire day in the noisy bounce house that is parenting.

$$\mathcal{C}\!\partial$$

My inner bartender is tall and looks a lot like Tom Selleck circa his *Magnum, P.I.* days. His mustache precedes him. He has eyes that twinkle at me and are full of promise. I can see every one of the bottles glowing on the shelves behind him—hues of amber and rose and gold—and they seem to be lit from within.

Always leaning on the bar, my inner bartender asks, "What'll it be?"

It's not impossible to have a bartender in your bathroom. He resides in the quiet places. Sometimes he meets me on my back stoop, but the birds distract him and I often find myself getting up and weeding the garden, or picking the last of the summer tomatoes.

We all have an inner bartender.

Some of them wave Visa cards at us. Others smile at us from behind a large display of baked goods. Others just talk to us and tell us what we want to hear. They are thoughtful because they reside, deeply, in our thoughts. They know us so well. It's a comfortable relationship. My inner bartender shows up when my triggers present themselves, and he beckons me, for a moment, to contemplate a heavy-rocks glass of brown liquid.

The other day, I tried to wedge in some writing time while my boys were at the pool. We were all enjoying the last days of summer, but I found myself increasingly stressed about finding time to write under a deadline while two very tan and squirrelly children pranced around me. The pool was a lovely solution. The water was soothing, and I could sit at my little plastic concession-stand table and madly type away while my boys pranced around, but over *there,* in the water. I was here, and they were over there. Occasionally, one would come over and ask for a snack and I would hand him some cash. It was perfect. So, I spread out my towel on the tippy plastic chair and opened my computer with a sigh of relief. And then, a little kid showed up.

He was not my kid. I don't know who he was. But he had no problem with personal space because, soaking wet, he came over to my table and rested his chin on his hand, staring at my screen.

"That's a comPUTER," he said.

"Yes." I kept typing.

"We have one of THOSE. MY BROTHER USETED IT."

This was a kid with a rather wobbly grasp on social norms and volume. He was dripping on my screen. I moved the computer over.

"I SEE YOU ARE DOING SOMETHING. WHATCHA DOING? WHAT IS THAT?"

I started looking around for his mom. Ah, there she was. She was smiling at me because this was a cute moment. Her son was socializing with the nice lady.

"Beat it, kid. I need to work."

I wanted to say that. I did. He was all up in my business, this little kid, and he was wet and started picking his nose. Then, his interrogation continued.

"IS IT A STORY? WHAT'S IT ABOUT? WHAT IS IT?"

And I was done. Nothing ticks me off more than redundant word usage.

This type of behavior is a trigger for me. Mild annoyance scratches at my brain. Triggers are not big, bad, obvious things such as the war in Afghanistan. The war in Afghanistan is horrible, but we can deal with horrible. Likewise, cancer isn't a trigger. It is a total asshole, but it's not a trigger. However, I have a friend in recovery who also has breast cancer, and the onslaught of books her aunt sends about beating cancer triggers her.

"I know she means well. And I know the books are probably great." She looks out at the distance and then back at me. "But damn. I just want to feel normal for five minutes. If I get another Amazon package, or a link in an email, or a Facebook post about this book or that . . . Did you know I have a stack of those books next to my bed? I can't give them away. I keep them. Because they are good, right?"

I told her to give them away. Maybe that was bad advice, but the stack of books can be rebought. Her sanity might need her to even take all the books out to the trash and dump them. If not, they might make her want to drink, and breast cancer was never cured by alcoholism.

That's what triggers do; they can make us act crazy.

They can make us talk to bartenders in the bathroom.

And they have no manners or sense of time. That little boy at the pool? He had me triggered at hello. And no, it's not like I was going to upend the tables and head out for the nearest bar. I have been in recovery too long for a trigger to ever make me drink at someone— at least not immediately. My triggers like to sit a little and percolate. They squirm and itch at me and make me long for space and a deep breath. They make me feel indignant: "Here I am, just trying to get some work done, and this is an IMPOSITION." I start upping my volume on choice words too, similar to my short table guest: "I don't DESERVE this. I need to get away. I need a break. I need . . ." and then the looking around starts.

I bang myself up against a whole list of things to soothe. I become a pinball in search of the lever that will divert the discomfort.

Triggers happen, and I still experience them. This is because it's a cold, cruel world with people who still don't know how to use the passing lane on the highway. It's a proven fact.

Brian and I travel home a lot to visit our parents and experience five minutes of nostalgia for the suburb that has a Bed Bath & Beyond every four hundred feet. When we do this, we often visit Fritz's, a restaurant that our boys love because we are good parents like that. It's a train restaurant where you dial up your order on a phone, and then a train comes and delivers it to you. It's magical when you are five. It's still cool when you are seven or eight, plus there is always ice cream. And when you're forty-six? Not so much. It's really loud. Those trains don't know how to deliver the food without making a whole bunch of racket, as trains do, and I find it rather distressing at times.

Parenting is really just an endless flowchart of decisions. Do you buy them the Pokémon backpack that costs crackamillion dollars, or no? Do you allow sleepovers when they rarely sleep, at all? Do you give in and let them watch a *Star Wars* prequel? In the grand scheme of things, this whole train restaurant thing seems like a harmless decision. It's loud, yes, but the chili cheese dogs are really tasty.

But one afternoon, after a long visit with family, we packed up and started to head out of town and decided to stop at Fritz's to buy our children's affection with chili fries. We arrived at lunchtime, all hungry and ready for the fun, and crammed ourselves into a red vinyl booth.

And that's when the restaurant decided to get mad at me.

It started with the chili cheese dog. It arrived cold and sad, an emasculated version of its former self. As I am an ex-waitress, I have it written in my moral code to never, ever complain about food, so I pushed it around my plate and felt sorry for myself. Also, my children hadn't had a decent night's rest in four nights, so their little brains were misfiring all over the place, and they were nutballs. For some godawful reason the restaurant also had a television positioned up by the grill, and, of course, it was playing SpongeBob because the children in this facility were not stimulated enough. My husband was really interested in something on his phone. The child in the booth behind us decided to kick his enthusiasm about the trains onto the back of my seat. And all the while, the trains chugged and clattered by at full volume. In fact, they exceeded the maximum.

These trains go to *eleven*.

I unstuck myself from the vinyl seating, gave the kicky kid behind me a death glare, and headed to the bathroom. As soon as the door swung shut, I pondered my reflection. It was quiet. No piped-in music, no SpongeBob, no trains from hell. It was just me, the mirror, and a bunch of buzzy thoughts in my head. It was perfect timing for my bartender to arrive.

ᶜᵉ

"What'll it be?" he asked, smiling. "Something to knock you out? Lift you up? Take you away? Make parenting, trains, and life in general fade softly into the background? Want something in a glass that will make you, I kid you not, feel like you are *in* a Bob Ross painting? Want puppies and kittens in a clear liquid? Want something with olives in it so you feel sophisticated? Or how about something with amaretto, so sweet it's like drinking a jolly rancher, so you can relive your freshman year? Want to remember an old boyfriend? Here's some red wine. Want to forget? I've got something for that, too. Want something brown and substantial? You can pretend you're Irish. Or how about you just go for some gin, and you're in a pine forest? I've got people and destinations and feelings here for you, lady. All. In. One. Little. Glass."

That's when I realized my inner bartender talked too much.

So, I fired him.

I don't need a bartender anymore. Triggers happen because they have a pack mentality, and life is full of people, places, and things that are scratchy and awful. We can't live in a bubble all the time. Often, I can, but only after 9:00 p.m., when I can finally, *finally*, take off my bra and get into bed with a box of vanilla wafers and Netflix.

Prior to that, life was all "Here, hold this problem for me." Life is annoying like that.

I used to meet with my inner bartender because I couldn't understand why my triggers kept happening. And I couldn't understand how to handle them when they did. My bartender often said things such as "You can't control your children. And maybe you need to lose twenty pounds before you go on vacation," or "Where are the kitchen shears? What kind of person loses the kitchen shears?" And he smiled all the while, placed his hands on the bar, and waited.

He was a terrible bartender and a total jerk.

I wish I'd fired him long ago.

Triggers keep happening because I cannot control the crap out of my life. And then I get mad that triggers keep happening, which triggers me.

And don't even get me started on hormones. Hormones are the carnival workers of humanity. They are mysterious to me. How did they end up all up working in my body? They are completely disinterested in whether you have an enjoyable experience on your ride or not. They just strap you in, telling you to keep your head low, and set you spinning. And then, within minutes, you are crying, laughing, or nauseated. Carnie hormones.

I don't think separate triggers actually happen at all, when hormones come into full play. I think, perhaps, just one big, huge, colossal trigger slowly digests all the other ones like a great hormonal amoeba of destruction, and from there on you are batshit crazy.

That's when you just need to say, "Well, folks, I'm out. I'm moving to a tiny house in Colorado Springs for a while. It's for your safety and mine. I promise I'll stay sober, although I do hope some hipsters smoke a lot of pot in the tiny house a half acre over, so I can live vicariously off the fumes. It's legal there, you know. And at the worst, I'll probably just hyperventilate from deep-breathing all that mountain air. I will return once this hormone ride ends. I made some casseroles. They're in the freezer. Good luck to you all."

When a woman hits menopause, all states should mandate that she get her own tiny house experience. They do this in Sweden, and their crime rate is super low. I think I read about that in *Martha Stewart Living*, so it's the law. I think it would help out healthcare and the divorce rates in the United States, too. And how about this: Menopause? Nope. Meno-*paid leave*. I can see it on a bumper sticker.

What we do with triggers is what matters. I once tried to explain this ideology to my infuriated five-year-old after he had a meltdown because his evil brother ate his Reese's Peanut Butter Cup. Honestly, I felt for the kid. This was a *serious* offense. But, as I sat next to him and he heave-cried into my shoulder, I explained, wisely, "It's not bad to get angry. It's what we do with the anger that can be the problem. And honey, I know you are mad, but threatening to drop your brother's candy stash into the litter box, while a creative idea, is just plain old revenge. And we don't do that. It doesn't help our hearts. Besides, it confuses the heck out of the cat. Is it food? Is it a litter box? That sort of thing."

I'm no longer out to get revenge on my triggers. Granted, when I first got sober I did pretty much whatever it took to stay that way. I fought dirty. I ate a lot of junk food, lifting crinkly wrappers up to the heavens and saying, "TAKE THAT, ALCOHOL. I SHALL SMITE THEE WITH SOUR PATCH KIDS. VENGEANCE IS MINE!" I plugged myself into whatever soul-soothing, mindless escape I could to get through another day. And after a while, the Sour Patch Kids ended up as a dessert option, not one of the four food groups.

It's all in the reaction. If Mr. Trigger rears his ugly little head and I shriek and swat at him like he's a spider, then that's panic, and panic does not heal. Instead, there should be some breathing, a few prayers, and maybe even a phone call or a text to reach out. In other words, there needs to be a little wait time before I react all over the place because then my reactions are a little less crash-and-burn. It's almost as though I need to imagine that all triggers must have a twenty-four-hour waiting period before purchasing, or something like that.

⌐ᴼ

Back in the train restaurant's bathroom, I decided that I had stared at my reflection in the mirror long enough. Another lady entered, and it was getting weird. I breathed deeply, said the Serenity Prayer in my head, and applied my lipstick, MAC's Lady Danger. Appropriate.

Then, I exited and entered back into the sideshow attraction that was my family trying to leave the restaurant. Charlie came up to me, all aglow, with an idea.

"Mom, MOM, I just went to the BATHROOM," he exclaimed, like there should be a prize involved. "And you know what? I think? You know what? Do you? Know?"

All children talk like this. They're not on drugs. It's just what they do.

I kept nodding and smiling because really I wasn't going to try to engage yet. Nothing had been said, and I don't think he would have heard me if I responded, anyway. SpongeBob was singing at us over our heads.

"I think this place is awesome. BUT. THEY REALLY NEED TO PUT TRAINS IN THE BATHROOM TOO. LIKE, TOOT TOOOOOOOOT!!! HERE'S YOUR TOILET PAPER! DON'TCHA THINK?"

Perhaps I spoke too soon about those drugs.

I No Longer Have the
Damn Time for the Following

(Triggers from a bunch of my recovery friends on social media)

1. "Marathon hang-outs, such as gathering before and after a dinner, or events that are used as excuses to get sloshed, such as football games and music festivals." —Ellen

2. "Welcome receptions, drinks, dinners at conferences. No, thanks. You don't miss anything important anyway." —Karen

3. "Children. Laundry. Clutter. Overwhelm." —Emily

4. "Work holiday parties and happy hours." —Katie

5. "Same!" —Jessica

6. "Family!!! I just say NO!!!!" —Jeanette

7. "First-class upgrades. I don't say "no" to them, because I've found other ways to make it fun and special (and it's still more comfy), but it's a trigger." —Ingrid

8. "Me too! I flew first class during my first month of sobriety and thought it was the universe playing the most cruel joke on me! And I think one of my

biggest triggers is listening to my dad tell his old drinking stories. It's weird because I was not even alive when he was having these experiences, but they make me nostalgic for a reckless fun that was never even mine to begin with." —L.P.

9. "Good news celebrations. I'm already guarded against bad news WTFs." —Betsy

10. "Boredom!" —Jan

And finally:

11. "Chuck E. Cheese's. That place is just awful." —Me

PART THREE

enough

"I never talked. Then, I drank and I talked all over the place.
Then, I quit drinking. And I had to learn how to listen."

—ME

CHAPTER FIFTEEN

HOW TO
be sad

If someone wants to talk to you and begins by asking if you are sitting down, you sit down.

You always sit down.

My sister called me at work. And then she started the conversation with the whole "sitting down" thing, and it all went downhill from there. She told me she had been diagnosed with breast cancer. It was Halloween.

I hung up the phone and stared into space, trying to figure out what to feel. I knew I should feel a lot of things: scared, sad, mad, or any combination of the three. Instead, what I felt was . . . nothing. I felt a blurred absence of any feelings whatsoever. And that was when I first thought something was seriously wrong with me in the feelings department.

I have dealt with depression all my life. In my teens and twenties it was a frenetic, manic brand. I remember some instances when I was nearly immobilized from anxiety or gloom, and then, in a span of an hour, I was over it. I had no clue what to do with sadness except to gather it in a soulful embrace, like I was Cindy Lauper in her video for "Time After Time," serenading it at a rain-drenched window. Plus, sadness was also kind of cool. I wore black. I listened to Yaz's "In My

Room" on repeat. Sadness and I were quite an item. I wore a lot of wine-colored lipstick and watched *Twin Peaks*.

But as I got older, every once in a while, the sadness didn't feel right. I wanted to wear pink. I was tired of trying to like Pearl Jam. And I would try to shrug it off, like my oversize flannel shirts, but the sadness would stay.

Perhaps I trained it to stay. I don't know. When all you do is listen to Radiohead's "Creep" on repeat for days, then maybe you rewire your synapses. Either way, sadness had slouched over to my futon and asked me, "Dude, can I crash?" I didn't know how to ask him to leave. It seemed impolite.

I dated a guy when I was in my late twenties who was cute, kind, and smart. He was the total package, if you're into that kind of thing. Nate was enthusiastic about KU basketball. For those of you not well versed in the best college ever, KU stands for Kansas University. He didn't paint his chest red and blue or anything like that, but our dating life involved attending a lot of games. And I did so, also enthusiastically, for weeks. I located all my old KU sweatshirts, put my hair up into a high ponytail, and channeled my inner cheerleader. I knew she was in there somewhere, buried underneath a decade of The Cure and loving inappropriate men. But about three months into the relationship, I found myself disenchanted. It was a lot of work, trying to be so perky all the time. Nate was so cheerful. He liked puppies, and he called his mom every week.

I found it exhausting.

I broke up with Nate and I never really looked back. I didn't find myself listening to Hootie & the Blowfish and missing him. But I *wanted* to miss him. I wondered what might have been. Would I have glommed on to the cheerful? Would it have finally sunk in enough to stick around?

In my thirties, I found Jesus. This phrase always makes it sound like he was stuffed under a couch cushion or something, but you know what I mean. My life found its center point, and it was worth celebrating. And I did, and still do, because grace deserves joy. Grace creates joy.

But I still got depressed.

I didn't really know why. I thought Jesus had it in his contract to fix that sort of thing for me, but as I came to find out, life is still hard.

Maybe it was because bad things happened. My grandparents died. My boyfriends left.

September 11, 2001, set me off into a lump of weariness for weeks. But with events in my own life—things a therapist would call "situational depression"—I experienced a weird state I can only describe as numb dread. This was what I felt when my sister told me about her cancer. It was like closing thick, dark curtains on a window and then sitting right in front of it, wanting to feel anything—warmth from the sun, rain, or a cold breeze. But instead, I felt mummified.

And then, I would get depressed for no reason at all. I mean, there's hormones. I know about those. And it could be a brain thing, some sort of chemical imbalance. This always makes me picture my brain with little tiny brainy arms all flung out, trying to walk across a balance beam with a lot of frantic waving and sometimes toppling over with a thud.

It's a seesaw of weird synapses. Tragedy occurs; I respond with grim acceptance. Commonplace events happen; I respond with hardcore despair that wrenches my gut and leaves me spinning. So, in sum, I prefer the big tragic events. Those hit me, and I descend, yet I feel relief. "This is doable," I think. "My sister has breast cancer, and I can function. I'm operating heavy machinery. I'm walking and talking. Look at me, depressed and still all vertical about it." It does drum up guilt, though. "Here I am, with a sick sister on Halloween, and I feel guilty about my constant self-regulation of this whole thing. I suck. What kind of sister am I? It's so depressing."

And on and on.

Overwhelming dread, brought on by no discernible reason whatsoever, is what I deal with today. Still. Even after recovery. Even after spiritual awakenings.

And even after marriage and children, which is supposedly the apex of womanhood and bliss—as fifty thousand mom blogs with all their cute jewelry and chalkboard memes will tell you. Parenting, in fact, can corner the market on woe. But I digress.

⁀

One afternoon not long ago, I woke up, got dressed, brushed my teeth, and sent my two cherubs off to school. Then, something in my stomach seemed to shrivel, and all I could feel was pain. It wasn't sharp or searing like the scorch of a burned finger from a hot pan. This was a dull thud in my gut. It crawled up into my throat and gripped hard.

I walked into the kitchen and wiped off the counter. I stared out the window. I walked into the living room and sat on the couch. I got up and got the mail.

I sat back down on the couch. I stared at my hands.

My house, it seemed, had filled up with water that morning. It felt like I was sinking. Chairs and couches and beds were spots onto which I could tether myself and get my breath. But everywhere else, I had to paddle. Just to get from one end of the dining room to the kitchen took what felt like Olympic effort, and I am a lousy swimmer to start.

This is depression.

And there was absolutely no reason for a flood. Outside, the sun was bright, and the day had the easy warmth of late summer. My bills were paid. My children were well-dressed and attractive. My pets were all fluffy and cute. The previous day, I woke up, dressed, brushed my teeth, and proceeded to walk through my day without even as much as a paper cut. Today, I was drowning in my living room.

And all the while, while treading water, I was trying to figure out where the water had come from.

Floods don't really make room in their schedules for this kind of analysis. They just pour water in all over the place, and you spend your time in other worthy endeavors like escaping. Figuring out how this all happened comes later when the insurance guy shows up.

Because sadness needs to mean something, doesn't it? If not, that's just cruelty, and this world has enough of that.

It's confusing. If I pay too much attention to depression, it grows. It's like a toddler who has to have the meltdown in the superstore. There are times when the only way to survive is to plod along with eyes averted while the kid wails about the Ninja Turtles cereal and rattles the bars of the shopping cart.

But then, if I ignore depression, it grows. And then, one day, it becomes the sullen teenager who sneaks out at midnight and gets arrested. The cry for help is real.

On my slowly sinking, depression days, I tend to find a spot where I can sit and watch the waves for a while, like my bed. Usually a cat or two jumps up to join me, and we stay dry for a bit. We wrap up in a blanket and watch the water rise, and I have a conversation with God that starts like this: "Really? Why? What now?"

I curl up onto my side. All I can hear is this echoed refrain in my head: "Oh, please. Please help. The water is so cold."

There is no big solution for depression. I can't pull some universal stopper and watch the waters recede to one final circling flourish around the drain. It's not easy or tidy, and any more water analogies are not going to wash it away. Medication can help, and yes, it's totally okay for people in recovery, even me. Journaling and exercise help, too. Counseling is always a good option if you can make sure to find a therapist who isn't creepy and doesn't ask for hugs when you don't want to give them. It's all so tedious and messy and depressing, dealing with depression.

This is where my children come in handy. I knew they would make themselves useful at some point, and in this case they've become like those therapy dogs. They can sniff out trouble within seconds, and then bammo, they're at your side, all wiggly with wet noses. However, their main therapy tactic is to annoy you into distraction by repeatedly asking for snacks with Ninja Turtles on them.

I cannot help but listen when my children are asking after me. Because that is all they seem to do: ask for things. Children so rarely come up and just say, "Why hello there, Mother. Lovely day, isn't it? Would you like some tea?" This would be grand, but it would also be weird, like my children had been replaced by a British butler named Barnaby, and butlers make me nervous. (Note: This is purely theory. I have never actually encountered a living butler, or even a dead one.)

Instead, their questions push and prod and require an answer, and unless I want to delve into totally horrible parenting, I try to avoid that even on my worst days. Common courtesy requires that I answer my children when they ask me thirty times that day, "Mom? Mom? Can we play Wii?"—if only to establish that no, for the thirtieth time, they cannot. Repetition is our love language.

ᶜᵉ

When I was drinking, I did not listen well. I chattered away and clattered about and turned up the music, and all the noise and ruckus kept me from really hearing anything at all. Until, of course, I was silenced by my own addiction, and no amount of noise came through. That's how alcoholism works. It works itself up into a great din with a crash of cymbals and timpanis. It's the final bars of some great opera, exuberant, loud, and long. But then, the music always stops. One way or the other, the music always stops.

My sad days would be poured into a glass when I was drinking, and lo, instant fix. The glass, and its contents, worked. I would pour a glass of Pinot Grigio, the music would swell, and relief would come. I didn't need counseling, or journals, or medicine, or God. I had wine. It did all the work for me.

Until, of course, it stopped doing any work at all. Wine, like duct tape, always functions well at first. But then it frays and gets all gummy and makes you look like a slob. But you rarely notice because, well, it's wine.

When I quit drinking, I was scared to listen. I was afraid I would hear things such as "You are the worst mother" and "You are never going to get better" and "Why try? What is the point?"

And when I quit drinking, that is exactly what happened.

Sad days would descend. And with them came a sick certainty that I was the worst mother.

I would never get better.

And there was no point.

When I listen to my children, I am in the habit of bending down and leaning in toward their faces. I know this makes me sound lovely and maternal, but really? My boys use these breathy, teensy voices at the weirdest times, and so I need to get millimeters away to just hear them. Incidentally, this tiny-voice thing sounds cute and all, but it only occurs when we are alone. If others are around, for example my pastor, or really anyone, my children like to bellow things such as "WHY DO THE BACKS OF YOUR LEGS LOOK LIKE THAT?" These types of conversations are often completely ignored, because as much as I advocate for common courtesy, I know better than to engage with them because I might kill them.

In my sadness, I picture myself leaning down and listening to me. I put my hand on my shoulder and look into my eyes and come in close. I can't carry any journals or a Bible or even a counselor's office number scrawled on a slip of paper in my hands because they are placed on the shoulders of the child who is me. My hands are full. I have no other thing to do but listen.

Because what else is there to do?

I could give up. You see, sometimes all the counselors and prayers and green juices and yoga classes don't seem to work. Or they only work a little, or for a little while, and it's all so very tiring to keep trying. So, I could give up. I know people who have, and they are dead. Perhaps it seemed their best answer to a brain so tired and tangled.

And I could keep drinking because that was an answer for a while. I could drink and drink, but soon that would prove about as helpful as slamming a door so hard against the winter cold that you break the glass. In comes the cold, and the only thing left to do is sit down and fall asleep in it.

I could give up. It might seem easier.

But when I started to listen to that girl, the one with the shoulders that shook with tears and anger, and I bent down and looked at her face and just listened? She looked right back at me, and in a still, small voice I heard her say, "I am still here."

Feeling Sad?
Refer to this Flowchart

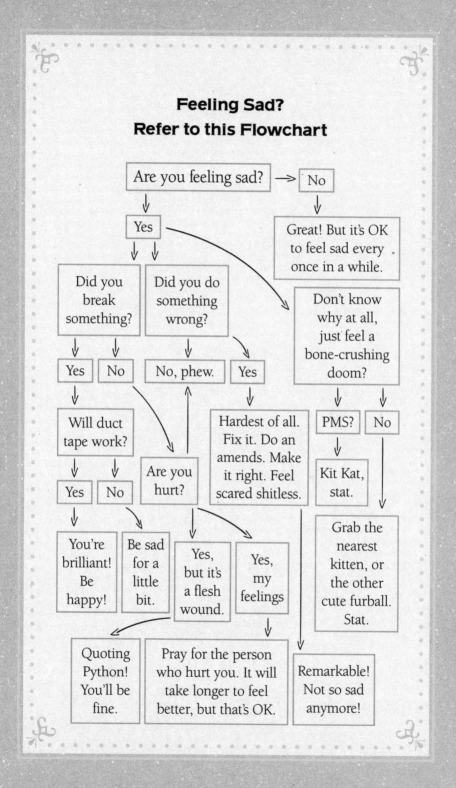

CHAPTER SIXTEEN

HOW TO
be happy

As I walked up the steps of the governor's mansion, a plainclothes policeman with one of those weird earpiece things greeted me. Next, he opened the door and gestured me inside. Mr. Plainclothes Policeman made eye contact, and immediately I was nervous. Then, I had that lovely moment where I remembered that I was sober, and I hadn't done anything with a breath of illegal in it for a long time. I smiled at him archly and sauntered in.

It was just like the set of *The Bachelor*—but for happily married people and without all the short skirts and contouring. I was wearing tall, very *Bachelor*-contestant-like red heels, however. They were patent leather and expensive, and I had bought them specifically for this event. I thought of them as my talismans of good luck.

In retrospect, I don't stand by my decision to wear shoes that make walking impossible. Shoes were invented to aid in the walking process, right? But these shoes? They had it in for me. As I wobbled past the front entrance, my spiky heel caught in the front rug and I did a lunge and clatter, right into the marble hallway. A small group of people stood in front of me, in full view of my acrobatics, and as they turned my way I realized it was the governor—the governor and a flock of authors. My shoes were total schmucks.

Being happy is hard. I fear its entrance because it has the potential to trip all over itself and not live up to my expectations. Also, happiness, like a perfect spring day, eventually has to leave, and I am so very bad at leaving.

As the people surrounding the governor stared at me, I began to think that it would be a good time to leave. Each person was holding one of those Jell-O-cup-sized plastic containers filled with wine. As I recovered from my entrance, smoothed my skirt, and smiled at full wattage, I did that thing where I tabulate all the alcohol around me. I was like an idiot savant with a drinking problem. I counted four reds and two whites in the circle, all still at three-quarters full. And there was some weirdo with a Coke. The governor had a glass of white, too, I noted. His was half gone, so of course I decided he had a "problem," and it would only be a matter of time before we started seeing articles about him like that poor Mayor Ford guy in Canada. I sidled up closer to Coke guy and smiled at him because surely he would be drinking at this event if he could, so he must have been one of my people.

It seems I look for my people whenever I am at places like the governor's mansion, about to talk about my book because it won a big award. It's a fabulous thing to win awards and schmooze with government officials and guys with earpieces and eat my weight in brie, but Lord, I am having the worst time.

I would love a drink right now. Well, it's the guilt-ridden, codependent, kind of Sid-and-Nancy kind of love, but anyway.

A young girl walked by in black pants and a green polyester vest. I gathered she must be hired help, since no one wears such attire unless under duress. She noticed that I was standing without a Jell-O cup and asked, "What would you like?"

Okay, Vest Girl. I'll tell you what I would like.

I would like to redo my entrance to this event because now I think everyone has decided I'm the weird one, instead of Coke guy.

Actually, I would like to have written a book and won all sorts of awards for it, but when it comes to actually standing in this room right now, I would like a hard pass.

I would like someone in recovery to walk up to me right now and say, "Let me take you away from all of this," hand me a Reese's Peanut Butter Cup, and usher me smoothly out of the room.

Also, I would like that person to be Robert Downey, Jr.

I would like to know that I will always be happy and successful.

I would like to get out of these shoes because they are slowly taking my toes and bending them backward on top of my feet.

I would like to stop smelling the sharp tang of red wine because now, as a woman in recovery, I can sniff out alcohol like some sort of bloodhound with a Big Book.

I would like to eat about twenty of those brie-and-puffy things. They look delish.

I would like to understand how I got here. And really? I would like to feel happy about it.

I finally told Vest Girl I would like a Sprite. It was fizzy and would have to do. I considered asking for a Shirley Temple, but that seemed precocious. I only do precocious in the privacy of my own home.

The floor in the governor's mansion was a slick, smooth, highly polished wood that had the feel of ice. I wondered how the governor and his wife walked in this house. I would imagine only super grippy things would work, such as rubber rain boots or those Croc atrocities. Then, an image of our governor in purple Crocs popped in my mind, causing me to shake my head.

Socks, on the other hand, would be a blast—all the careening and swooping about—because you could travel from room to room at light speed. A new mental image formed of our governor doing that epic Tom Cruise slide into the living room in *Risky Business*. I shook my head again. I then wondered whether the rooms upstairs were carpeted. There, I could walk from one end of the room to the other without any mishap. I longed for the upstairs. To my left was a long stairway leading up to the thickly carpeted wonderment that was the second story, but Mr. Plainclothes Policeman might not understand my fixation on flooring.

I went through all of those thoughts in about twenty seconds.

No one, besides our dapper waitress, spoke to me.

I clearly needed to sit down. Talking to people was next. The waitress showed up with my Sprite, and I wondered if I could just strike up a conversation with her. "So . . . what brings you here?" That sort of thing. Instead, I walked, very, very slowly, over to a side room. It seemed to be a lovely and airy sun porch with vases of sunflowers and yellow wicker furniture. It also had a precarious step down to enter, but the flooring inside there was a slate that didn't seem as deadly as the front entrance.

I carried my plate with a polite amount of cheese and my Sprite and concentrated on making it to a chair. Everyone in the room was chattering away, like they all liked each other, and I smiled. Smiling is easy. I can do smiling.

And then, one gentleman saved my life. "Come sit here! We are all trying to get over being awkward and introverted authors with each other. Come be introverted with us. Who are you?"

I would have kissed the man if I hadn't been so carefully trying to walk toward him.

ᒧ

My book, *Bottled: A Mom's Guide to Early Recovery,* won an award from the state and was named a Kansas Notable Book. The other books that had been selected were all about Kansas trails or birds or historical things that happened in our state, which were respectable topics and kind of what I figured academic and virtuous people read.

My book was about being an alcoholic. It described crying jags, throwing carrot cakes, and my longing for tequila at 3:00 p.m. Here, at the governor's mansion, I had the whole "One of These Things Is Not Like the Other" as my walk-on theme song. There were numerous introductions and interviews and all of them were paired with "So, your book is a bit different in that . . ." and I would smile, nod, and wonder whether next time I should insert some prairie wildlife with drinking problems.

I was thrilled to win the award.

It was a huge honor.

ᒧ

On the next night during the awards ceremony, I found out that I would receive a medal. My kids watched, big-eyed, as the governor's wife placed the heavy accessory around my neck. Their mom won something blingy. It was a good moment.

There were other good moments. My best friend, Christy, came to the ceremony and took all sorts of pictures, like best friends are supposed to do. She sat next to me before I was supposed to go up and collect my award because I was nervous and she makes me laugh.

"Do I have stuff in my teeth?" I whispered to her. "Is my hair okay?"

"Cool it," she whispered back. "You look fine. Just whatever you do. Do. Not. Fall. Down."

As far as friends go, Christy is top-notch. In fact, later, when I was chatting with her on the phone about my uneasiness at the cocktail party, she gave me the best advice.

"Dana. If you want a Shirley Temple, order the damn Shirley Temple."

"Really?"

"Yes. Just say, 'You there, sir! Bring forth a Shirley Temple!'"

"Uh, 'bring forth'? This isn't a jousting event."

"Whatever. Say it!"

"Bring forth a Shirley Temple!"

"Good! Now, again!" We practiced this for a bit until it got weird, and my husband yelled from the next room, "OH, GO GET ONE, ALREADY."

At the awards ceremony, my boys and my husband sat farther back because small children needed to be far away from the pomp and circumstance. The ceremony was held in the state senate at the capitol, in a room spacious and official and historical. Everything seemed touched with a sort of glow. I was a big deal on this day.

The previous night's cocktail party, with its talking and tricky flooring, was but a memory. Today, I got to walk around with a flipping medal around my neck like I had won the Book Olympics. After the ceremony, our handler even said to us, "Now, we want you to keep your medals on all day. Please. So everyone will know you are who you are." Evidently, introverted authors don't wear medals often, and every year they always nervously try to shed them as soon as the award ceremony has ended. Silly authors. She would have none of it.

"I'm supposed to wear this all day," I told Brian, shyly looking down at my medal like I needed to get permission.

He hugged me and said, "They're taking a picture in the rotunda with all the other big, famous authors. Go on. We'll meet you by the entrance. The boys want to mess with security and play with the metal detectors."

I came to find out, when you forget that you have a large metal object the size of a coaster hanging around your neck, security detectors scare the living daylights out of you. It's a learning process.

I got home from my weekend of me and put the medal in my office. My office is where I have all my writing files, books, and other professional trappings, and so of course I never, ever really, actually write up there. I write on the couch with a bag of Blow Pops and my dog as a blanket. It's a process.

On those days when the cat boxes are overflowing and I burn the quesadillas, I miss my medal. I wonder if I tromped upstairs—past all the detritus of life, small children, and other nuisances—and put it on, whether it would protect me like Wonder Woman's golden bracelets. Maybe it could ward off overdue bills and insults from online trolls with a flip of my wrist, perhaps paired with a Wonder Woman karate kick. Given my lack of grace, this might end up with me hurting myself, but the image makes me smile. For one day, I was fabulous, and *I have a medal to prove it.*

It all takes me back to my inner showgirl. Now, I have bling to add to my strut. "Me?" I snarl, "I am a WRITER," and I prance away, medal thwacking me in the chest, trailing glitter and validation.

Happiness is hard. It doesn't stick around. It squirms away, and then all we have are memories, and those don't stick around either if you're old like me. Happiness is effervescent. Bubbles aren't stalwart. If they were, they would *hurt.*

Happiness is hard because it dresses itself in big emotion, and this can tire a person out after a while.

Happiness is hard because it doesn't follow a rule book. Some days, it doesn't make a lot of noise; it can approach as silent and slinky as a cat. On other occasions, it wants to party, and we can sing along. Other times, it seems to want to alight on my hand, but if I grip too hard, it dies. I cannot handle all this willy-nilliness with the happiness.

In other words, it is not easy keeping happy alive.

Grim despair seems a little more dependable. It can be dialed up with the weather, family dinners, or a government election. It comes when called.

I remember happiness when I was drinking. It had an elevator feel, like my head and heart were full of helium, and the world, with all its necessary troubles, stayed below. It did come on cue. It served me like that Vest Girl at the governor's mansion whenever I opened a bottle. But eventually, this version looked down at itself and rebelled. "I'm on break," Happiness would say. "This vest makes me look really stupid. I'm out." And just like that, she would be gone.

So now that happiness and wine were refusing to work together, I would have to serve myself. Happiness is such a pain in the ass.

I remember drinking and being happy. And then I remember drinking *only* so I could be happy. It's like booting up your computer and telling it, "Now, you will be the one thing in my life that will bring me wealth and riches! Nothing else can contribute to this. Only you, my darling computer, will show me the money. Not a job, or investments, or hand-crocheted potholders at a craft fair. Nothing else will WORK. It's all on you. Okay!?"

Silence from the computer. "Okay, maybe we don't have to aim for being rich. You can at least help me buy some new shoes without tippy heels, right?" And the computer would stare back at me. It would be a one-sided conversation.

"Or, uh, just help me pay the bills? So the lights stay on? Please?"

I remember happiness when I was drinking, but I don't trust these memories. They feel all John Hughes-y with puffy sleeves and too much Drakkar Noir. Or, I recall gleaming bars, dark-red lipstick, and martinis like I was some sophisticated nineties Bond Girl. I know those kinds of things happened, but mostly? It was just me, some boxed wine, and tater tots.

I'm pretty sure drinking wasn't happiness. Even from the beginning, drinking for me had an ulterior motive, and I don't think happiness operates that way. It doesn't have time for motives; it's too busy taking up all the space with its own happy self.

My husband, the weirdo-normie, got to have his share of happy drinking shenanigans. I don't hold it against him. He has told me many times, "I just like the taste of beer." In my view, this is the equivalent of the people who say they read *Playboy* for the articles. But Brian is not much of a liar. He gets all blinky when he does, and as I recall, the last time he did drink a beer it was one of those atrocious, coffee-thick Guinness things. That kind of beer takes real commitment. So yes, it's possible he really did drink it because he likes the taste. Who else would down a glass of molasses-flavored foamy booze? So, he had fun. He did stupid stuff and partied with his friends and, I think, once, bull riding was involved.

For me, drinking always had a subtext. If Brian's drinking was an Adam Sandler film, mine was one of those Ingmar Bergman numbers with all the pale people and subtitles.

I didn't even know what happiness was then. If someone had delivered a basket of puppies and chocolate—perhaps separate baskets, let's be prudent—to my front door, I might have felt an upward blip in my emotional matrix, but I wonder.

And, as I got older, I smushed any chance of happiness under all that wine. Maybe we all lose bits of our happiness as we get older. Maybe it gets smushed under being responsible or getting a big house or being the perfect mom. I'm not saying we are all happiness-smushers, but I don't know. Have you waited in line at a big-box store recently? Have you looked around? *Nobody seems all that happy anymore.* My brand of happiness just got smushed a lot faster due to all the alcoholic stuff. I am a cautionary tale.

This is the part of the book where I stop and blame Donald Trump for all of this, but I'm not going to. Besides, everybody else has already done that.

Instead, I blame Charles Schulz.

Yes, you know the one. Beloved animator. Snoopy maker. The one who told us, "Happiness is two kinds of ice cream." But happiness is so *not* that. Because, eventually, we're going to wonder where all the mocha chip is. What's that green stuff over there? Does it have sprinkles? Why did *she* get sprinkles, and I didn't?

Thank you, Charles Schulz. Thank you for selling us the idea that happiness can be bought with five crayons and a glance from a red-headed girl. *Well, it's not that easy, Charlie Brown.*

Happiness is hard. It's elusive and shifty. It can alight, all diaphanous and soft, like a veil, and then poof, someone grabs it and runs. It usually gets ripped in the process and then is impossible to mend. Veils don't stitch up properly. They're too . . . veil-y.

And no, all of you who are going to say, "Well, contentment, then! We just need to feel contentment. Happiness is like the super buzz you get the first half hour after you take your allergy pill! Contentment is just the knowledge that you won't be snotting all over the place for twenty-four hours. Let's just stick with the boring consolation prize that is contentment! Right?"

Oh, no. Wrong. Very wrong. I am so tired of hearing people try to sell contentment. Yes, contentment is a deep-seated, blessed assurance that life, despite its nuttiness, will essentially be okay.

But I want to be happy. I really, really do.

And that's why I'm going to say I can only handle happiness with God's help. Otherwise, I mess that crap up.

Yes, many of us believe that God is in charge of a peace that is hunkered down in our souls. I know this. I feel it when I slow down, sit outside on the back stoop, and watch my new kitten, Willie, attempt to catch butterflies. That's a soul-cleansing kind of peace. It's the "It's a nice world, after all" kind of thing. Willie glances over as if to say, "Hey! Look at me! I'm generating calm and contented feelings in your soul right now because of my cuteness! We should do this every day! Meet me out here tomorrow!"

Incidentally, the butterflies might not feel quite the same about all this, but I do notice also that Willie has goofy aim and precision, so there's that. But as I sit out there, feeling the sun and drinking my fourteenth La Croix of the day, I often wonder about the same thing.

Am I happy?

That's precisely where I go wrong. Happiness gets cagey when you try to analyze it.

I give it to God and ask, "Could you, um, help? I have no idea, still, how to be happy. After all this time—even with sobriety, healthy children, and all of it—I know I should feel thrilled beyond belief."

God doesn't answer me when we talk like this. It is so annoying. Instead, I sit for a bit longer, go inside, make some goulash or something else my children will pick all the green bits out of, and go to bed, asking, "Well, see? There you go. Another day and I don't remember any happy. What is the point? Why am I here, then?"

Did you know? If you ask, "Why am I here?" often enough, God will answer. Here's how.

He'll give you a feverish kid with a sore throat who sits with you in the big recliner in his room until midnight, even though he is a bit too big for this.

He'll give you a sick cat that has to have surgery for a blocked urethra and then has to be bathed and carried around for days afterward because he keeps peeing all over himself, you, and the floor. And while you carry his huge, furry, white self around, he looks up at you with such sweet patience that you stick your face in his furry chest, and you don't even care that he smells really bad.

He'll remind you that people everywhere have hurricanes and floods and fires. Displacement and fear and loss are all around. You will help how you can.

He'll remind you that you could drink over all this existential pondering of your own life, but you don't. You don't ever drink over it—because that's not an option anymore.

And that's when you realize that you are really, really happy about all of that.

Happiness doesn't need to be folded up and put away with some faded ribbons, hair clips, and tiny, sparkly jewelry from my past. We think that's where happiness lives, in the past, in the slanted sunlight of playtime with a tea set and some Barbies. And maybe it's true that happiness did really partake in that tea, but I would venture to say that it was just as flaky there as it is here.

The last time I flew, the plane landed as the sun set. As we slowly descended, the clouds were a lovely apricot and deep blue, and I pressed my nose to the thick glass of my window and stared. It was like those fireflies. The sunset only lasted a few minutes, but what if it had been there, smacked up against my window, for the entire trip? I bet eventually I would have looked away. And I certainly wasn't going to suggest that we take the plane for a few more swoops around to keep the sunset with us a bit longer. I do have control issues, yes, but trying to pilot the plane is where I draw the line.

Happiness, maybe, isn't *in* us, just waiting to be released like a bunch of doves at a wedding. It's like those clouds that we flew through out there, all lovely and God-breathed. We traverse through it. It's not in our jurisdiction, and that's what makes it so cool.

What if, when the plane landed, I stomped and wailed like one of those unhinged travelers you hear about on the news. "Bring it back!" the nutball lady in 18C cries. "Make the sun set again!" I would have been looking at a TSA holding cell within seconds.

Life is too short. I had sick kids to hold and a cat to try to administer a pill to, which in itself requires an act of God. And as long as I remember them, I will, dare I say it, be happy. Or, happy-ish. And I'm content with that.

Definition

Happiness: (noun) a state of being in which you find yourself feeling extra-good. Sometimes this feeling is attached to a specific event. But sometimes it's not. And other times it shows up at totally inappropriate times, like when your kid gets sick at the holiday choir concert and almost yaks all over the risers. You can up and leave while all the moms give you sympathetic looks, but the reality is that you get to go home to your pajamas and watch *Elf* with little Mr. Sickie. Mainly? Happiness is elusive. I wouldn't take it home to meet the folks, speaking truthfully. It's shifty.

See: contentment—happiness's less hot, but more reliable, big brother.

CHAPTER SEVENTEEN

HOW TO

say no

AND HOW TO

say yes

"Honey, could you . . ."

"No."

"Just, sweetie, I . . ."

"*I SAID* NO."

I decided to practice saying no. And Brian wanted to know if I could pass the salt, which I was handling like a boss.

Saying no used to be hard for me, even though it's only one wimpy little syllable. I didn't say yes well either, actually. I just tried to duck and run and get out of all obligations in a sneaky way, which would leave me feeling embarrassed over my inability to utter one-syllable sentences. It's an identity thing. Along with my Super Sobriety Girl cape, I also wore the Perfect Mom wrist cuffs, and don't even get me started on Smart and Sexy Wife bustier. That thing was uncomfortable.

It's hard to accessorize so much. Most days, I'm good if I remember to wear a bra.

No one told me about the mantle you would wear when you became an adult. There's no real ceremony with it. No audience claps politely for you while some dude in a cap and gown places the ceremonial "you are a big grown-up" garb on you. But still. It's on there, draped across your shoulders in all its glory, pressure, and satiny seriousness. I mean, really? Could there not have at least been some balloons and a cake?

Or some money? Graduates get cash in envelopes. Instead, I put wads of cash in envelopes and send it to school in my boys' backpacks because our lunch money is always overdue.

When you are a full-fledged adult with children and a mortgage to prove it, you're responsible for so many things.

Fun Fairs. Fun Fairs are neither fun nor fair, but they happen a lot, and you will be volunteering at them.

Pets that die and then you have to tell your kids. I'm not sure which event is worse.

Somewhere, at some point, a kid will vomit on you. Repeat.

Lost bills that are really, *really* important. Like, State of the Union kind of important. If you don't find that bill, you will end up in a van down by the river.

Lost kitchen shears. Still. Totally lost. I refuse to buy a new pair because I cannot accept that I lost them. How? People lose hair ties and bills but not big kitchen shears with red handles. Those shears and their disappearance are a symbol of how far I have sunk in terms of organization. I could write a book on those shears alone.

Sex that is really borderline mundane and might, just maybe, possibly, be filed under "It's been two months, so let's give this a whirl, okay?"

A solid knowledge of Ninjago's characters. Their development. Their arc. The pathos. I laughed. I cried.

Moments in life that seem to come up at you and go, "Gotcha! Bet you don't know how to handle this one at all, do you? But you have the mantle, so go on now! Good luck!" You decide to walk out there while you look back at all the other adults, who are standing there nodding and waving you on. However, you are completely clueless and just want to grab a fuzzy blanket and a nap.

Ugh. All this nonstop adulting. It is for reasonable people, and I kind of think reasonable is overrated.

ᑲᕋ

One of my favorite bands is the Flaming Lips. They don't do reasonable. If you have ever seen this group live, it's kind of like an acid trip. I've never had one of those, but I like to think the Flaming Lips will take me there without the scary hallucinations. Their performances are often paired with grown men in furry costumes and sparkly lights. The music is ethereal and lovely, and all the while the lead singer is dressed up like the Cowardly Lion.

This is so spot-on.

I tend to think people like this have a firm grasp on reality. Wayne Coyne knows exactly who he is. He's a dude who likes to dress up like a Teletubby on some days. That takes some verve, and he's got it. The man really does not care. And if he wants a parade for being an adult, he just puts on a drum major costume and throws his own. This speaks to me.

There is not any time in my foreseeable future when I will don a costume and throw my own parade. But I like to think that Wayne does this stuff because he has reached a level of Wayne where his insides match his outsides.

We all should be so lucky.

When I got sober, I worked hard on myself. This involved dealing with other people, because I don't live in Antarctica. All that work didn't get tossed when I drank again, but it did need some retying of the knots. I needed to learn, again, how to say no and how to say yes.

No, really. This is some really hard stuff.

Saying no means we have to be brave. Saying yes means we have to be willing. Both are hard as heck.

None of this is possible unless we know who we are. That's the trouble with adulting. We're so busy being all adult-y and trying to be perfect that we forget.

Not long ago my eight-year-old had a fabulous idea, and he decided to make me a thank-you card. The card itself was under duress, I have to admit. We have chore sticks, a collection of popsicle sticks in a cute little mason jar that I wield as a threat to my children whenever they bludgeon me with "Mommmmm, I'm booooored." Voilà! The Sticks of Pain!

I saw it on Pinterest.

Anyway, one option is "Write a thank-you card." Charlie was thrilled because other sticks in there are all about cleaning bathrooms, and I watched as he gathered paper and crayons. Then, because I am a Mom and I spy on things, I saw it.

"Dear Mom. Thank You For . . ."

I smiled and walked away. My work here was done. My kid was taking a moment to thank me for being his momma. I had reached high parenting.

About thirty seconds later, he brought me his card. On the front was a stick woman with snakes sticking out of her head. I wasn't deterred. All the pictures my children draw of me look like this. The front read, "THANK YOU MOM."

I smiled. And then I opened it, and it said, "YOU BUY ME THINGS." And there was a little stick child playing with his stick Wii.

"Oh, okay. You're welcome?" Backstory: Charlie and Henry were in the middle of three days of grounding from any sort of screen time. This was a great consequence that worked well for the two or three days after they got the Wii back, until I grounded them again. So, the card was perhaps a subtle dig at his third-world-country existence at that point.

But also, really? What about all those nights I spent with him, sitting in the recliner, with all those sore throats? What about the endless Band-Aids and kisses and advice about communicating with his brother without smacking him with a baseball bat? And hey, what about childbirth? Huh? That was a toughie, and I never once complained to him about it. To his father, yes, but not to him.

Now it's true, Charlie is a little mercenary. He likes cash. So, this thank you was pretty sincere, I think. But it bugged me. I had in my mind—when will I learn?—that my identity as a mom was a bit more salt of the earth, not Bank of America.

You see, I thought he had me down as something different.

Identity. It really only works if you play only with yours and refuse to share. I think identity behaves best when it's off doing its own thing. If it keeps going up to others and asking, "How does my personality look today? Does my identity fit well in these jeans?" it ends up sounding neurotic and insecure. Nobody wants that.

I thank my relapse. It gave me the gift of identity. It taught me who I was, and who I wasn't. Relapse tore off all the covers and left me bare. And then it said, "Get dressed, woman. And this time, choose what you like, not what you think everyone else wants you to wear. Okay?"

So, I took my time and I chose.

Comfortable jeans. Not super skinny ones. Those are for moms on Pinterest with the big felt hats, and I look stupid in both.

Bright-orange running shoes. I will never get shot by a hunter while jogging.

Red lipstick. Sexy underwear once in a blue moon. Mostly Hanes.

Often a book. A lot of times a Bible. Always my laptop.

My wedding ring.

My laughter.

Possibly a Blow Pop stuck to my butt.

Coffee cups with kittens on them. Not real kittens, though.

I really don't care anymore about what other people see. My identity has a lot to say, but the conversation is just for me. Finally. FINALLY. It's no longer a constant sending out of who I am to the masses, hoping the masses will like me. What do the masses know? They all like fidget spinners.

My identity prior to sobriety was like that freshman kid who selected communication arts as his major. This degree is a way to communicate that you don't really know exactly what you want to do with your life, but you want to do something with your life. So, it's a start. I didn't really know what I wanted to be as a mom, a teacher, a writer, or a wife. I had ideas that my "mom-ing" would be super loving and soft voiced and richly layered with Jesus and fun crafts. My "wife-ing" would be the same, crafts included.

And my teaching and writing? Someday there would be a movie made about me, telling how I inspired so many children to write their way out of the inner city, but I think it's been done. Plus, I teach in a small town.

Also, I kind of pictured myself as a tiny-house person. They're so cute.

My identity now kind of thinks those tiny houses are nutball.

In fact, my identity is not tiny at all. No one's identity should be. We are too big for that.

෴

I don't know what happened, but somewhere along this road I found I have big feelings about things. I have hard yeses and nos about life. My addiction turned me inside out. It left me empty. And I am so grateful for that emptiness, because then I could attend to my soul without any distractions. It was like learning to samba in a large, empty ballroom as opposed to my crowded living room. I was an echo chamber, and my soul wasn't taking any crap anymore. Life was too short to dink around with indecision or apathy about anything. I stand with my decisions. I do that a lot. Standing. Shoulders back. All good with being me.

This makes me sound rather intense but with really good posture. It's not like I go to the store and strut through the aisles saying, "Yes! I choose YOU, Bartlett pears! You spark JOY! I KNOW WHAT I WANT, AND IT'S PEARS!" or some such thing. That's a little much, even for me. But I am a lot better at saying no and enjoying it.

I don't say no to every Fun Fair, I promise. (Note: Actually, that's not true. To date, I have not ever volunteered at a Fun Fair. Come at me, PTA.) But there is an endless pull and tug of motherhood and all its trappings that come my way. So often, these requests are festooned in the soft, pretty colors of "But this is what moms do," and I just smile and turn away. From some of them. Not all, just some.

The other things I say yes to, and it's a really happy, full-on yes.

It's funny, but the more nos I utter, the bigger the yeses become.

I would love to explain that this means I am now donating a lot more of my time to service, the church, and a whole lot of other worthy endeavors, and yes, sometimes it does mean that.

But what I would also like to touch upon is sex.

Puns are so easy when it comes to this subject.

Sex is not simple. I am a sober woman, married for over ten years, and also somewhat hormonal. I wish I could say that sex was as simple as my Netflix queue. You click on a few options. Quick comedy? Romantic drama? *Game of Thrones*? (No. Just, no.) And then, boom, it's the best-preprogrammed seven minutes of your life.

Instead, sex is a mystery but without any death or cops. Maybe like a nice, cozy *Murder She Wrote* episode. I never quite know how it's going to end. But somehow, along the way, I started to understand my marriage more. I stopped trying to be what I figured Brian wanted, and I just loved him.

A lot of times this didn't involve the bedroom at all. I didn't wonder anymore whether Brian was disappointed in me if I couldn't take on another Sunday school class or messed up our schedules for the weekend. Long ago I would have mulled over this for a good hour, at least. But now, if he asked me to pick up his dry cleaning and I couldn't, I wouldn't "sorry" all over him and offer to reroute my entire day to accommodate. I would say, "I can't today," and then watch how the world, and our marriage in it, did not end.

The better I became at my nos with him the better he could see me. And, miraculously, he loves me all the more for it. I know this because I just asked him, and he blinked a little and said, "Yes. I love you all the more for it." I believe him.

I didn't worry about whether our sexy time was on par with what *Men's Health* tells you is needed in a relationship. When I stopped looking at sex as a task to prove my great-wife status, I started having it because I plain old wanted to. True, our sexy time usually involves at least one cat on the bed, a very concerned Hosmer whimpering outside the door, Saturday morning cartoons for the children, and a small window of time. But we're like the Navy SEALs. We are stealthy, and we get the job done.

My marriage is a cuddly one. We lean in to each other, often, and our boys roll their eyes as Mom and Dad make out while cleaning the kitchen. We are comfortable and content, and I think we kind of look like one of those ads for Viagra, all happy, serene, and cutting vegetables, which you know is code for we are going to be getting it on soon. We don't really need the Viagra, at least not yet, so that's a bonus. I think the state of our marriage is due to a lot of things: Brian's affable spirit; our love for God; a lot of baked goods; but also, all my yeses and nos.

I am able to say, "No, I refuse to quit on us" and "Yes, I am staying right here" while we travel through it all. I say things like "No, I don't like it when you stay up too late and watch too many documentaries about World War II. Yes, your knowledge of artillery and tanks is impressive, but you are totally grumpy. Cut that crap out." And then, a few minutes later, "Yes, I love you. Always."

In fact, my nos are more prevalent than the yeses. Who would have thought?

"No, I don't drink anymore."

"No, I listen to myself first now."

"No, I am going to stay right here, with me."

"No. I will not ever, ever give up."

Say Yes or Nah?

Just Say Yes

1. The neighbor kids' lemonade stand.

2. Bell ringers. Make eye contact, smile, and give them your money.

3. Any old movie that casts one or more of the following: Cary Grant, Jimmy Stewart, John Wayne.

4. "Dancing Queen" by ABBA. In any situation.

5. When your cat interrupts your writing to come sit on your lap. When this occurs, you are achieving peak human. You shut your computer and commence petting. Always add an extra five minutes if there is purring.

6. Long, weirdly detailed conversations with your children that occur when you are tucking them in and you are really tired.

7. Charlie Brown television specials. Stop and watch. Do not move. I repeat. Do not move until done.

8. Naps.

9. Spending the birthday money that your mom still sends you even though you are an adult on a face

cream that costs crackamillion dollars and smells like grapefruit and angels.

10. Doggie kisses. Dogs never have weird motives or power issues; their kisses are pure. Their breath, not so much.

Nah, Don't Do It

1. Spending that birthday money on groceries like you think you should.

2. Volunteering for something that makes you feel all droopy or tense. Despite what the PTA might tell you, assisting with events that make you feel droopy and tense are not good for schools or families.

3. Those time-shares when you have to listen to the guy talk first. Unless something about this gives you a secret thrill, which means you are a special type of person and I'm not sure I understand how to write for you.

4. News shows where people speak like they're not yelling at each other, but really, they're totally yelling at each other.

5. Conversations with my husband that start with "Do you smell that? Come 'ere."

6. Flamin' Hot Cheetos. I might catch some grief for this one, but my God, people. That color of orange is not meant for our insides.

7. Points. From places like Walgreens, CVS, or Target. I probably have about five hundred thousand points all over the place. PetSmart. Lowe's. Bob's Bait Shop. Endless points and emails, and now they're actually texting me about all the money I would save if I would come to their store and spend more money.

8. Couponing. It's only for the few, the proud, and the medicated.

9. *Flavor of Love.* Not seasons one and two, though. Just season three. Total train wreck.

10. Alcohol. When offered, I politely decline: "Why, no thank you. Last time I drank I ended up in Vegas with a tattoo of Condoleezza Rice on my face, and it takes like a handful of concealer to cover that sucker up." And then, I smile mysteriously and saunter off into the sunset.

CHAPTER EIGHTEEN

HOW TO

cry

AT A

coffee shop

So, this is my life. It is messy, and it is mine.

Right now, I am holding a tiny black-and-white kitten with stubby legs on my lap, and we are conversing about life. When I walk past him later he crouches and wiggles his bottom, ready to pounce. His pounce is light as a feather, but I react in the same way I do when my kids high-five me: I overreact, and the kitten looks proud of himself.

It's a lovely little moment.

And now it's about five minutes later, and I realize I've locked myself out of the house.

I blame the stupid kitten.

I am on a writer's retreat at a friend's house. It's a parsonage, next to a tiny little country church. Flowers and fields surround me, and I have three days to write, sleep, eat, and repeat. But right now I am staring at a door, my hand pressed to my lips in frustration, and tears fill my eyes. My computer, my writing, and my life are inside that house. And I am out here.

The kitten saunters by, and I swear I see him shrug.

I call two friends. They are not home. I search the gravel. I pace. I curse. This was supposed to be this idyllic, perfect weekend in which I finish my perfect book, and here I am, crying and sitting on dusty lawn furniture. It's really hot, and evil kitten has now decided to take a dump in the grass in front of me. Such is my life.

I start to plan. I could go find a hotel and some paper and a pencil. I could go back home. I could just sit here and cry and pet cats. There are many of them, and they have slowly been approaching me like cute little farm zombies, slowly stalking and surrounding me.

I locate my wallet and car keys in the car because I have just been to the store. One must have certain provisions when writing, such as Froot Loops, peach-pear La Croix, and the ever-present Blow Pops. It's about ninety-nine degrees in the car, but I slump in the seat, trying to figure out my next move. Nothing comes to me. So, I go sit with the cats, and they want to press their bodies up against me and purr, but it doesn't help. I had one precious weekend to finish this book, and I am totally screwing it up. I am a miserable pile of misery.

And here comes the self-talk, stomping through my head like a boorish marching band.

"How could you do this?"

"Why are you such a flake?"

"What's the point of writing a book about screwing up if screwing up makes you not write the book?"

That last one makes my head hurt, so I kick some gravel.

Finally, I remember to pray. I drop my head to my chest and I pray. "Please, Lord. Please. I've got nothing here. Can you please, please, PLEASE show me the key?"

And then, I stand up, walk back to the car, the one I have already searched from top to bottom four times, and open the back door. And there, on the floor, is the key.

I grab it. This is a *moment.* God is so good! I am going to finish the book! Everything is going to be all right!

And then, I lean up against the car door and promptly lock my keys and wallet inside.

Perfectionism is my way of combating fear. I fear that I am not enough. I fear loss or pain or rejection. I fear having to sleep in my car overnight because I lost my keys.

Most of my fears tend to hang on to other people. This is pretty common unless you only fear sharks or spiders, which are totally legit but sort of one-sided. My fears bounce back and forth between me and other people, and I watch it all like some sort of neurotic tennis match.

But after I've figured out who I am in all of this, I put down the racquet. The fears come and sit down next to me. We drink some water and maybe talk a bit. They don't always offer a high five and say, "Well, I think we're all done here! Great match! Cheerio!" and walk off into the sunset. It's not perfect, but it's better.

When Brian arrives with the keys—after almost a two-hour drive—we sit out on the back stoop and watch our boys and the kittens. I lean up against him. Brian has joined the hipster brigade and has grown a glorious red beard. He looks like a Brawny ad, and he smells like coffee and bacon. The beard is still new, so I get to play the lovely game called "Hey! It's a New Husband!" every time I kiss his scruffy face. This weekend, as he walks toward me from the car, I have forgotten he has one. So that is a bit of an extra thrill.

I have missed him.

I sigh into his shoulder, which is solid and warm. "I messed up. I'm sorry," I say.

He shrugs. "I don't mind. We got to drive the Flint Hills. Nothing's better than that on a Sunday afternoon."

"I kind of thought the book was doomed." I gesture back to the house, where the book waits.

"Nah. It's just another chapter."

My boys come toward us. Henry is already covered in dirt and holding Tipsy, the little black-and-white one. Tipsy is special. He was born with a deformity that has shortened his legs, and he is also not the smartest cat on the block. But Tipsy has no clue about any of this. He lies back in Henry's arms, squeaking at him. Henry still has his morning breakfast all over his shirt and face, and he has lost his shoes somewhere in the grass by the back shed. This is normal for Henry. Shoes are his nemesis.

Henry looks down at Tipsy with total adoration, and I do the same with Henry. They are perfect.

They are perfect not because of what they do. They are perfect because they are loved.

Perfection does not lie in what we accomplish or feel or do. It is seated with the love that we give ourselves and others. Perfect love casts out all fear. To me, Henry is perfect. Charlie is too. And if I can so vehemently believe that for someone else, then it only makes sense to believe the same for me.

ᶜᵉ

Full circle. Again. My writer's weekend is in the same town where my alcoholism started to really ache and grow. I migrate back to the same coffee shop where I used to nurse a hangover. Here, this weekend, I write about my life with all its blessings and its work and its ephemeral happiness. I write about enough-ness, which makes happy tears come. The hipsters stare, but I cry anyway. Soon, I will wipe my face, locate my keys, and head home. Once more into the imperfect breach.

It's a perfect ending to the continued beginning that is me.

❧ ACKNOWLEDGMENTS ❧

Acknowledgments are lovely and terrifying at the same time. Lovely because it is only through the help and wisdom and just plain spoiling of others that I made it here.

Terrifying because I know I'm going to leave someone out. If I do, please know I am old and tired and just wrote a bunch of pages and it made my brain hurt and what's next for me might be a nice home somewhere and soft foods. And whenever I say "You know who you are" in this—that's you.

I want to start by saying a big thank you to Central Recovery Press, and especially to Patrick Hughes, who had to field so many emails that started out like this: "This might be a really stupid question, but . . ." Bless you. Thank you so much for allowing me into the CRP family.

Also, to the lovely and so very talented Janet Ottenweller, who actually and willingly read this book multiple times and managed to keep cheering me on. She is responsible for 90 percent of this book. I just wrote it. She made it shine.

And thank you, Eliza Tutellier, for introducing me to this whole world of book publishing and helping me not freak out about it. You are a peach. A very calm and supportive peach.

Thanks to Marisa Jackson for the best cover design in the history of cover designs. You get me and my vision. Which is very hard, sometimes because I am so weird.

I want to thank my tribes. I have a lot of them. Amy and Jenna and Alissa—thank you from the bottom of my heart for your encouragement and coffee and love. And coffee. Always coffee.

Christy. You are, quite simply, the wind beneath my wings. Sing it, girl.

Meredith, Katie, BK—my holy trinity of faraway friends—thank you for being who you are. You have shaped me and connected me to all the things good in this world.

Thank you, Marlene, Tina, Dawn, and Cindy for my daily God-shot.

Thank you to all the women who are REAL. And hilarious. All at the same time. You know who you are.

Thank you, BFB, for allowing me to vent, whine, shout, sing, and dance a happy sober dance whenever I please. You are always there, and it's such a comfort. And thanks to my daily BFB gratitude group—I lurk; therefore, I learn.

Thanks to Stefanie Wilder-Taylor. You started this whole thing. You really are a Big Deal.

Thanks to my church. You know me, and you love me anyway. And to Pastor Darrel, Pastor Jeff, and Pastor Jeremy, my three amigos? You teach me about grace and surrender. I owe you, big time.

Thank you for my little twelve-step group. I love you guys. ODAT!

I want to thank my sisters. Nobody gets it like you do. Jenni, Sherry—you mean the world to me, and I love you!

Brian, you were the first one I wanted to call when I got my first article placed in a magazine for real money! Thank you so much for your support and your grace—more today than yesterday.

Thank you to my boys, Charlie and Henry. Your momma loves you. Please don't read this book.

And, of course, Mom and Dad. Thank you so much for all the love, wisdom, and support. I love you so.

God is faithful.